MW00640143

David Hölter and Peter Fronteddu

Making Leather Knife Sheaths

Volume 1

·4880 Lower Valley Road, Atglen, Pennsylvania 19310

Other Schiffer Books on Related Subjects:

The Lockback Folding Knife: From Design to Completion,
        978-0-7643-3509-9, $29.99

Basic Knifemaking: From Raw Steel to a Finished Stub Tang Knife,
        978-0-7643-3508-2, $29.99

Making Integral Knives,
        978-0-7643-4011-6, $29.99

Making Hidden Tang Knives,
        978-0-7643-4014-7, $29.99

Originally published as *Messerscheiden Band 1 Köcherscheiden: Von der Konstruktion zur fertigen Lederscheide* by Wieland Verlag GmbH.
Translated by Ingrid Elser and John Guess
Cover design and layout by Caroline Wydeau

Schiffer Books are available at special discounts for bulk purchases for sales promotions or premiums. Special editions, including personalized covers, corporate imprints, and excerpts can be created in large quantities for special needs. For more information contact the publisher:

Schiffer Publishing Ltd.
4880 Lower Valley Road
Atglen, PA 19310
Phone: (610) 593-1777; Fax: (610) 593-2002
E-mail: Info@schifferbooks.com

For the largest selection of fine reference books on this and related subjects, please visit our website at **www.schifferbooks.com**

We are always looking for people to write books on new and related subjects. If you have an idea for a book, please contact us at proposals@schifferbooks.com

This book may be purchased from the publisher. Include $5.00 for shipping. Please try your bookstore first. You may write for a free catalog.

In Europe, Schiffer books are distributed by
Bushwood Books
6 Marksbury Ave.
Kew Gardens
Surrey TW9 4JF England
Phone: 44 (0) 20 8392 8585; Fax: 44 (0) 20 8392 9876
E-mail: info@bushwoodbooks.co.uk
Website: www.bushwoodbooks.co.uk

Revised Design by Stephanie Daugherty
Type set in Courier Std/Frutiger LT Std

ISBN: 978-0-7643-4015-4
Printed in China

CONTENTS

Contents

A FEW WORDS UP FRONT

Knifemaking as a hobby is becoming increasingly popular. More and more people are discovering how much joy it can be to create such a pretty yet practical device on their own. And of course, a pretty knife needs a quality sheath—at least with fixed blades. In addition, many knives manufactured in series only come with rather simple sheaths. A high-quality, handmade sheath can increase the value of every knife. Working with leather is also a pleasure and doesn't pose unrealizable prerequisites. Everybody who is a bit skilled can make a leather sheath on their own.

With this volume, we tackle the topic of knife sheaths for the first time. We introduce four different types of quiver-like leather sheaths with different designs and different technical solutions. In a later volume we'll turn to other types of leather sheaths.

Through this workshop series we would like to help you with all technical questions and spare you quite a few errors. This series of books assembles a multitude of themes all around knifemaking in a way which enables you not only to follow each step but to do it yourself, too. We especially emphasize the usability of these volumes in the workshop.

Thus all the volumes are provided with a wire binding. This way, the book stays open when you put it down. Also, we made the size of the images and fonts big enough to be visible and readable when the book is lying next to you while you are working.

We have tried to explain every step of work in the most comprehensive way. But before you pick up your tools, you should read through all of the descriptions and explanations in this book first. This way, you'll know what to expect and won't be confronted with unpleasant surprises later on. Use the materials and tools lists to put together what you need in advance.

My heartfelt thanks go to David Hölter for his great commitment—he never shied away from working long hours in the evenings. Peter Fronteddu once again captured every single step meticulously with the camera. From more than 1,000 photos we have tried to assemble a selection which depicts the sequence of work step by step.

And now I wish you much fun and success with your work!

Hans Joachim Wieland
Editor in Chief, *Messer Magazin* (*Knife Magazine*)

Knifemaking is one of the most diverse of all crafts. But what use is the best knife without proper packaging? So, to every handmade knife there belongs a proper protective casing. Dressing handmade knives in precious leather has a very special appeal to me. Whether it's the ancient handicraft of working with leather or the leather itself is hard to say. Perhaps it's the challenge of making a fitting and good looking leather sheath which brings the owner a lot of joy, in addition to its usability.

I hope that by means of the production examples and working techniques described in this book we can give you a few ideas, building blocks, and solutions for your own personal projects. And I do hope that working with leather sheaths will provide you with as much joy as it does for me.

A very special thanks to Peter Fronteddu, who composed the photos of all the work steps like a master.

David Hölter

BASICS

1.1 The Right Leather Sheath for My Knife

For the design and construction of a leather sheath for a fixed blade there are various possibilities. Depending on the type of knife, several given facts have to be taken into account in order to make the best leather sheath possible. In this book we will describe in depth the making of leather sheaths, their design features, and ways of producing them. We will introduce different variants to show a system with which a proper leather sheath can be made for almost every knife.

We will show the execution of each work step manually, mainly because no machine can reproduce the right feel necessary for processing leather. The actual realization nevertheless is up to each sheathmaker. We see this book less as a manual for special kinds of leather sheaths and more as a means of providing our readers with the basis for the realization of their own ideas.

Knife sheaths are more than just means for transporting knives and storing them. Quite often they are individual pieces of art, tailored to the person carrying the knife, his/her knife, and its needs. In this book we can only mention the basics, since the unlimited possibilities for personalizing are far beyond the scope of this volume. We nevertheless invite you to set your own creativity free and to implement your own ideas without restraints. The basic requirement for a knife sheath is the safe and reliable accommodation of the knife. It has to protect the person carrying the knife from inadvertent injury from the sharp edge while at the same time protect the knife from external influences. From these requirements arise some important aspects which have to be taken into account when designing and constructing a knife sheath.

1.2 Choice of Materials

Since times immemorial, leather has been a desired and versatile material. By means of different techniques for tanning and enhancement, unique characteristics and surfaces can be achieved, dependent on demand. Leather can be hard and stiff like sheet metal or soft and smooth like velvet—a unique product of nature.

1.2.1 Choosing Leather for Leather Sheaths?

For leather sheaths, all kinds of leather with sufficient stiffness and hardness can be used. Especially recommended is leather which was tanned by means of plants because this kind of leather, contrary to chemically tanned leather, doesn't contain any aggressive ingredients like chromium oxide which could lead to corrosion of the knife. After tanning, leather is divided into several parts. The central part, the back, called croupon in professional language, is the best and most expensive piece. It measures between 26 and 39 square feet (8 and 12 square meters) in size and usually is further divided into halves according to the

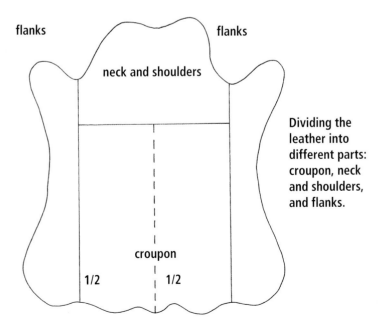

flanks   flanks

neck and shoulders

Dividing the leather into different parts: croupon, neck and shoulders, and flanks.

croupon

1/2   1/2

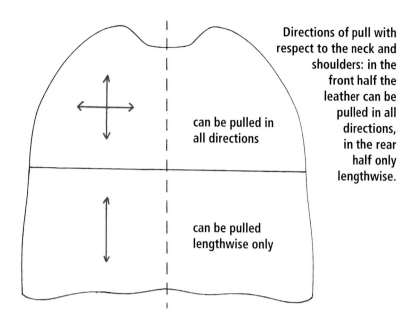

Directions of pull with respect to the neck and shoulders: in the front half the leather can be pulled in all directions, in the rear half only lengthwise.

can be pulled in all directions

can be pulled lengthwise only

length. The croupon is characterized by its extensive and consistent structure. The front part includes the neck and shoulders. It's about 2.6 to 5.2 square feet (0.8 to 1.6 square meters) in size and is characterized by its versatility of use. The flanks have a very slack skin structure and are thus used for lining and other parts since the material is under no stress or strain.

In this book we will discuss processing polished leather necks and shoulders tanned by means of plants—these materials have optimal characteristics for leather sheaths. Besides that, it is very forgiving with respect to processing and enhancement. It can be obtained with thicknesses from 0.078" up to 0.196" (2 up to 5 mm).

While cutting to size, the direction of pull has to be taken into account. The leather's direction of pull depends on the original skin structure and its quality with respect to strain. In particular, for leather sheaths with belt loops and straps, the parts which are subjected to tension have to be cut at an angle of 90° to the direction of pull. Thus a later wear-out of the straps is avoided. The rear half of the neck and shoulder section fits the

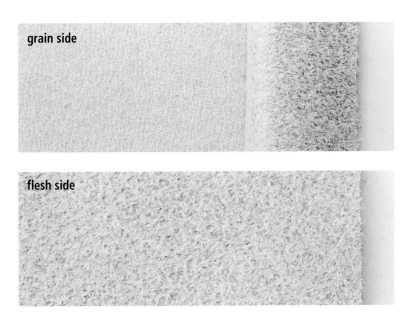

Grain and flesh sides of a smooth, full-grain leather neck with especially dense structure.

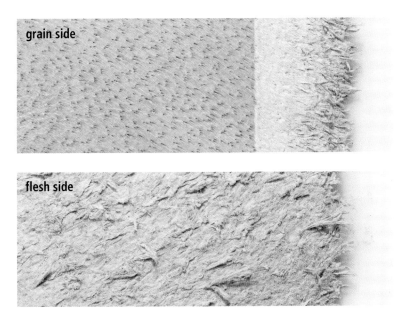

Grain and flesh sides of a smooth, full-grain leather neck with loose structure, not suited for leather sheaths.

purpose especially well because the direction of pull is length-wise to the neck. On the front part of the neck, in contrast, the leather can be pulled in all directions. The front part is thus especially suited for leather sheaths with separately added belt loops or straps because it can be shaped extremely well.

1.2.2 What to Look for When Buying Leather?

When deciding on the proper kind of leather, special emphasis has to be put on the quality of the leather. High-quality leather makes the job easier and guarantees that the piece of leather work fulfills its duty over the course of many long years. While shopping, you ought to look for a dense and tough structure on the flesh side (bottom). By no means should it (the underside) be loose and fringed. Additionally, grain side (top surface) and flesh side should form a solid unit and not separate from each other.

1.2.3 Which Thread is Best for Sewing?

Different materials are available for sewing leather. Natural yarns like flax, hemp, and cotton, but also sinews, have been used from ancient times. Modern threads made from plastic fibers have replaced them for the most part because of better quality. So-called "trout yarn" (for tying fly lures) is often used because of its high tensile strength and its interesting looks. Trout yarn is a braided yarn made of 10 to 20 strands and is offered in different strengths and colors. Plastic sinew made from a multitude of waxed filament yarns is also often used.

1.2.4 Which Type of Adhesive for Gluing?

For gluing leather so-called contact adhesives are especially suited to the job—these are adhesives that only stick after initial drying and putting the parts together. To use these adhesives, the parts of the leather surface which have to be glued together are first roughened, then the contact adhesive is spread thinly and

For gluing, dyeing, and impregnation, the workplace is covered with paper.

evenly onto these parts. After the initial drying, the parts are put on top of each other and are then pressed together with fingers or by means of slight blows with a mallet. If the glue contains solvents, a properly ventilated workplace is absolutely necessary!

1.2.5 Which Leather Dyes for Coloring?

For coloring leather, spirit dyes work well, but wood spirit stains can also be used. Prior to dyeing the leather, the color should be tested on some leather remnants. For this, a small piece of the leather used for sheathmaking is cut off and colored with the leather dye. After drying, the test piece is impregnated the same way the leather sheath will be in subsequent steps. Impregnation usually enhances the colors and also makes the leather slightly darker.

1.2.6 Which Method of Sealing the Cut Ends?

To keep the leather from fringing around the cut ends, a special kind of protection is needed. For this purpose, edge sealant based on shellac, pure shellac, or waxes like beeswax or carnauba wax are suitable. In addition, these substances cross-link the leather fibers and improve the resistance of the cut ends to mechanical wear and tear.

1.3 The Tools

1.3.1 Preparing the Workplace

For a working area, a wooden table with a chair and a good lamp will do. For cutting the leather, a wooden or plastic board is necessary, and for thinning a smooth plastic board or stone surface.

It is important that the surfaces don't have any sharp or pointed corners because these could lead to unwanted scratches on the leather. For gluing, dyeing, and impregnation, the working area should be covered with paper. You should always clean up meticulously because metal dust and shavings might cause dark stains in the leather which can't be removed.

1.3.2 Cutting Tools

In leather processing a multitude of different tools is used. Some of them can be found in every household, some can be obtained from specialized dealers, and others you can manufacture yourself, if necessary.

Among the cutting tools, the *shoemaker's knife* is the most well-known. It has a short blade which is about 0.078" to 0.118" (2 to 3 mm) thick. Most times it is sharpened on both sides, but there are also variants with an edge on the right or left side used for special tasks.

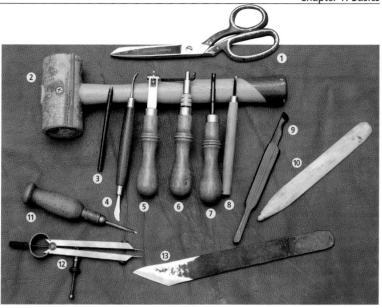

(1) Light leather shears, (2) rawhide mallet, (3) 3 mm (0.118") drive punch, (4) modeling tool, (5) space marker, (6) adjustable groover, (7) edge beveler, (8) V gouge, (9) handmade modeling tool, (10) bone folder, (11) scratch awl with handle, (12) wing divider, (13) shoemaker's knife.

The *scratch awl* is available in different sizes and is chosen depending on the diameter of the thread. It has a diamond-shaped cross section and is attached to the awl handle. The scratch awl has four sharpened bevels at the tip in order to cut precisely and without using much force.

Leather shears are strong scissors with fine to coarse teeth to hold the material while cutting.

The *edge beveler* is a special tool for breaking the corners of the leather. It is available in different sizes, and chosen depending on the thickness of the leather and radius of the corners.

The *V gouge* is also used for cutting linoleum. In leather-working it is mainly used for embedding seams.

The *adjustable groover* is used for shaping grooves at a specific distance from the rim of the leather. Most times it is used for ornamental grooves or for embedding the seams.

All cutting tools ought to be as sharp as possible in order to cut the leather without creating fringes.

1.3.3 Shaping Tools

The *bone folder* is one of the most important tools with respect to leatherworking. Quite often it is made from bone, but horn or plastics are also used. Usually the tool has a round and a pointed end to shape the leather. You can also easily construct this tool yourself. A variety of differently rounded bone folders is often helpful.

The *modeling tool* is also a versatile auxiliary for shaping. It can be obtained in different variations.

For *rounding the edges,* a handmade tool made of horn or bone is used. At the tip it is fluted by means of a round file and sandpaper so the edges of the leather can be rounded nicely.

You have to take care that none of the shaping tools have any sharp or pointed corners. The surfaces ought to be polished so you won't cut the leather inadvertently during work.

MINI-LEXICON

The most important expressions

Cleaning out: removing uneven parts and fringes

Skiving: partial thinning of the leather towards the cut ends

Sheath blade: the part of the cut leather which will cover the knife blade

Flesh side: bottom surface of the leather

Welt: inlaid part which prevents the knife edge from cutting through the seams

Grain side: top surface of the leather

Embossing: decorating the leather by means of tooling stamps

Twining: twisting of filaments into threads

Handmade modeling tool for leatherwork made from horn.

1.3.4 Other Tools

One of the most important tools is the *harness needle*. The special thing about it is that it doesn't have a sharp tip but is rounded. This prevents the thread from being cut when we are sewing back in the opposite direction. The needles are available with different diameters and different lengths, straight or curved.

The *space marker* is used for marking the distance between stitches of the seam and is available in different variations. Most common is a set with exchangeable wheels and various distances between spikes. The space marker can also be used for ornamental mock seams.

Drive punches and *hollow punches* are tools for punching holes or creating small plates. Drive punches are made from round stock and they have a milled ejection opening at one side. They are manufactured with hole diameters from 0.039" to 0.393" (1.0 to 10.0 mm) and are especially suited for punching small holes. Hollow punches and also wad punches generally are drop-forged and are recognizable by means of their "ears," which frame the ejection openings on two opposite sides. They are available from a diameter of 0.196" (5 mm) upwards. The larger diameters are mainly used for punching small plates. There are also special shapes available such as ones with oval openings or partly open ones for punching certain construction parts.

PROJECT I:
Quiver-Like Leather Sheath with Integrated Belt Loop

2.1 Planning and Design of the Leather Sheath

Our first project is a sheath for a plain straight, fixed blade knife without a guard. We will construct a quiver-like sheath with an integrated belt loop of polished leather dyed black that is 0.098" to 0.118" (2.5 to 3.0 mm) thick. We draw the leather sheath onto paper and thus create the design (a template can be found on page 136).

2.2 Creating the Template

To design and construct the template, we first draw a centerline onto the paper. We put the knife with its back flush to the line and draw the rest of its contours with a pencil.

From the polished leather, cut a strip that is about 0.393" (10 mm) wide as a measuring strap. Starting at the rear part of the handle, where the sheath will end later, measure the circumferences. For this, the strap is wrapped around the handle and pressed together at its front end. Let the end of the strap overlap by about 0.314" to 0.472" (8 to 12 mm) and mark this position on the opposite side of the leather strap. This results in the size of the necessary circumference plus the addition of 0.314" to 0.472" (8 to 12 mm), twice for the seam on both sides.

Measure the length of the leather strap with a ruler. Half of the resulting value is drawn onto the paper template from the centerline outwards at the position of the measurement. This procedure is repeated at the front of the handle, the end of the blade, and its center. Each time we transfer the measured values onto the drawing.

MATERIALS AND TOOLS

Materials:

paper, letter size
smooth, full-grain leather, ~11.8" ×
    5.9" (30 × 15 cm), thickness
    0.098"–0.118" (2.5–3.0 mm)
black, trout yarn, ~10 ft (3 m)
contact adhesive
plastic wrap
black leather spirit dye
1 pair of disposable gloves
black edge sealant
leather grease with beeswax

Tools:

1 drafting triangle
1 pencil
1 paper scissors
1 cutting board

1 shoemaker's knife
1 bone folder
2 harness needles, size 2
1 adjustable groover
1 edge beveler, size 3
1 space marker, distance between
    spikes ~0.196" (5 mm)
1 V gouge
1 scratch awl, width ~0.118" (3 mm)
1 handle for scratch awl
1 base for piercing
1 small sponge
1 cigarette lighter
1 pair of pliers with smooth jaws
paint brush, width
    0.393"–0.59" (10–15 mm)
1 shoe brush

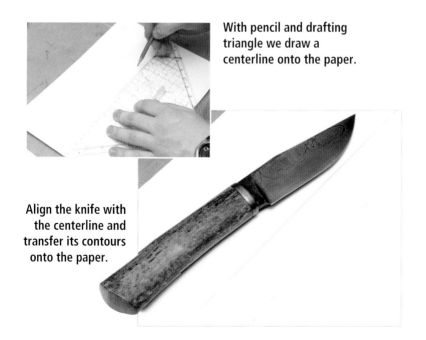

With pencil and drafting triangle we draw a centerline onto the paper.

Align the knife with the centerline and transfer its contours onto the paper.

19

Cut a measuring strap from leather that is the same width as the leather sheath.

Measure the circumference of the handle with the measuring strap and add 0.314" to 0.472" (8–12 mm) for the seam on each side.

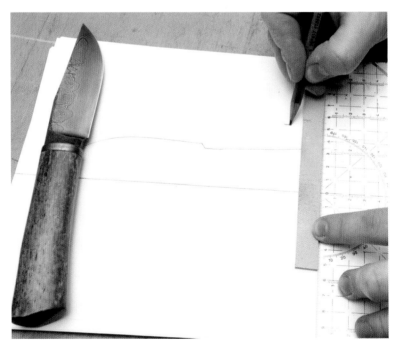

Transfer half of the measurement onto the template with the drafting triangle.

Measure the circumference at the front of the handle and transfer the values.

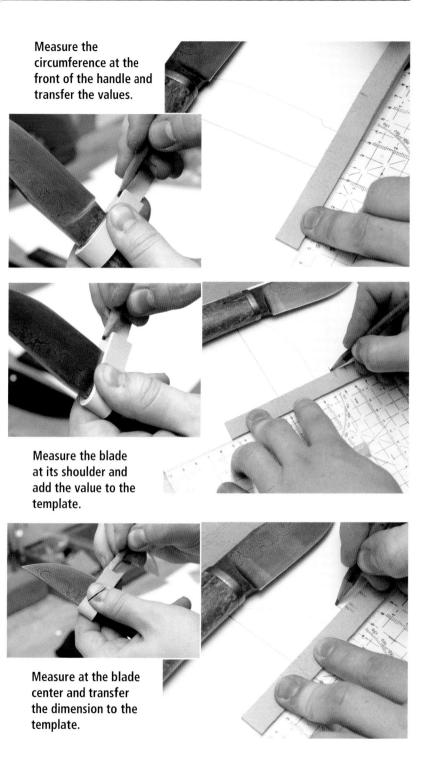

Measure the blade at its shoulder and add the value to the template.

Measure at the blade center and transfer the dimension to the template.

Now we connect the marked positions with an elegant curve. While doing so, you have to take care not to draw the curve inside these boundaries. At the blade tip we draw the outline with a distance of about 0.314" (8 mm) from the edge of the template.

Since the end of the knife handle is slanted, we copy this design element for the sheath opening. We measure the angle at the handle butt and transfer it onto the paper template, resulting in a harmonious transition with the upper end.

Connect the measurements with an elegant line while taking care that the resulting curve doesn't lie within the points of measurement. Towards the blade tip we narrow down to a width of about 0.314" (8 mm).

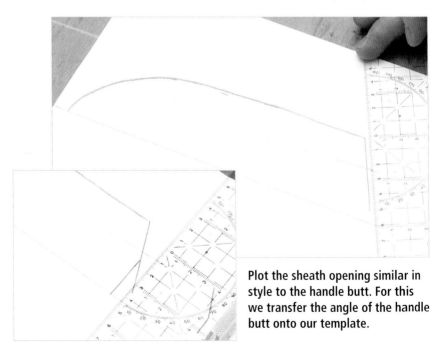

Plot the sheath opening similar in style to the handle butt. For this we transfer the angle of the handle butt onto our template.

For attaching the sheath to the belt, we decided on an integrated belt loop. The maximum width of the belt is set to 1.57" (40 mm). We transfer the width of the knife handle minus 0.078" (2 mm) on each side onto our own paper template. After that we draw two lines parallel to the centerline through our marked positions. The necessary length for the belt is drawn: 1.57" (40 mm) plus about 0.59" to 0.787" (15 to 20 mm) for bending back the loop.

To position the belt loop, we put the measuring strap around the handle at the point of the sheath opening. We mark the handle width, adding the dimensions of the seam, then transfer the measurements onto the template.

Draw two lines parallel to the center line through the points of measurement.

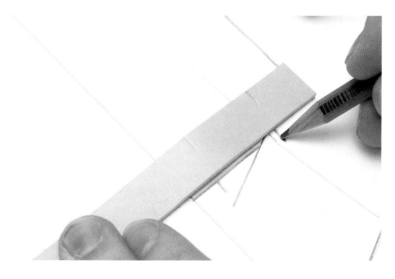

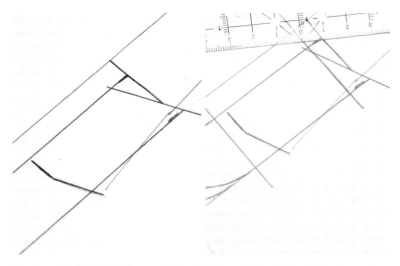

The length of the belt loop, with added length for folding it backwards, is entered on the template and the tongue for sewing on the belt loop is drawn.

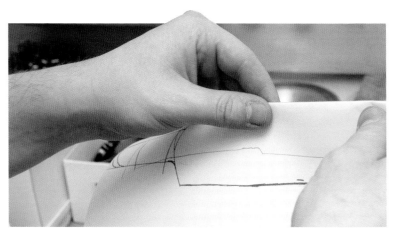

Now fold the template along the centerline.

In order to sew on the belt loop later, we draw a slightly curved tongue. Now we fold the paper template along its centerline and cut it out with the scissors. The pattern is folded open again and the second, superfluous belt loop is cut off along the line of the sheath opening. With this, our template is finished.

Cut the template along its contours with scissors.

The second belt loop is cut off along the contours of the sheath opening.

2.3 Preparing the Parts for Construction

As sheath material we use smooth, full-grain leather from neck or shoulder with a thickness of 0.098" to 0.118" (2.5 to 3.0 mm). While cutting, you have to take care of the direction of pull as described in chapter 1.2. To clearly show our markings in the photos we used felt pens, but drawing with a pencil is recommended to avoid coloration of the leather.

After drawing the outlines onto the leather we first roughly cut out the sheath blade by means of the shoemaker's knife. Then we cut the contours precisely. In doing so, you have to take care to cut cleanly and hold the knife vertically. We check the correct measurements of the sheath blade by folding it and putting the knife inside.

Put the template onto the grain side of the leather and draw the outlines.

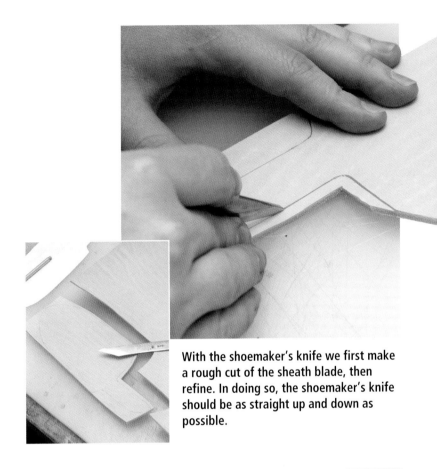

With the shoemaker's knife we first make a rough cut of the sheath blade, then refine. In doing so, the shoemaker's knife should be as straight up and down as possible.

The cut sheath blade.

Place the knife inside the sheath blade and check the seam allowance in the dimensions.

On the grain side of the leather cut a groove at a distance of about 0.157" (4 mm) from the cut end with an adjustable groover. With the edge beveler (size 3), clean the edges of the leather. At difficult spots and tight curves we use the shoemaker's knife. We also break the edges of the flesh side, but only in the area of the belt loop. The remaining parts are cleaned later on, after sewing the leather sheath. With the adjustable groover we also cut a groove on the flesh side of the tongue.

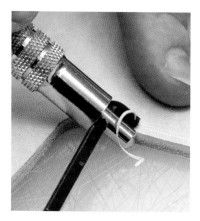

Cut an ornamental groove with the adjustable groover along the sheath opening and the belt loop.

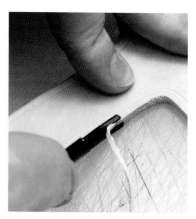

Cut the edges off with the edge beveler.

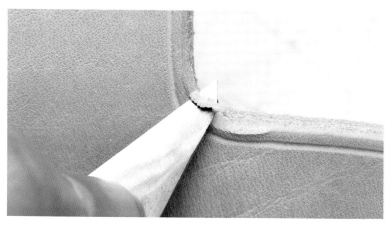

You may have to refine tight curves with the shoemaker's knife.

Work on the edges of the belt loop from the flesh side. Leave about 0.393"–0.787" (1–2 cm), towards where the seam will be later, as is.

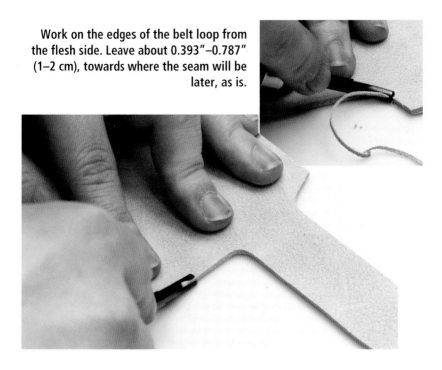

For the seam, and as an ornamental element, draw grooves on the flesh side of the belt loop.

Now we moisten the leather with a wet sponge. After a few minutes the water is absorbed by the leather and we can start to round the edges. For this a handmade modeling tool (as described in chapter 1.3) is especially well suited. By means of the resulting frictional heat and pressure, the leather fibers are hardened.

With the sponge we moisten the belt loop. After the water has been absorbed, we round the beveled edges on the flesh side.

For rounding the edges we use a handmade tool.

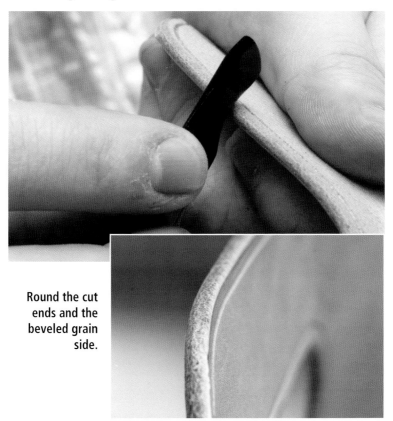

Round the cut ends and the beveled grain side.

2.4 Creating the Belt Loop

With the shoemaker's knife we skive the leather's grain side at the tongue of the belt loop down to a thickness of approximately 0.059" (1.5 mm). Smooth plastic or stone is a suitable surface to work on. Bend the belt loop backwards and position its end on the sheath back. With the awl we mark the tip of the tongue on the sheath blade.

For fixing the tongue we use contact adhesive which we dot sparsely. After initial drying we put the tip of the tongue onto the mark and press the glued areas together. If some of the adhesive smears or drips onto other parts of the leather, the glue has to be removed immediately. Otherwise this will result in bright spots when dyeing the leather later on. The adhesive can best be rubbed off with the bone folder.

The grain side of the tongue is skived down to a thickness of about 0.059" (1.5 mm).

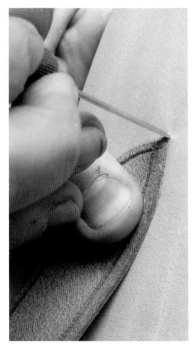

Bend the belt loop backwards and adjust.

Mark the tip of the tongue on the sheath blade with the awl.

Apply contact adhesive on the inside of the belt loop with a brush.

Bend the belt loop backwards. The contact adhesive is thus spread across the leather.

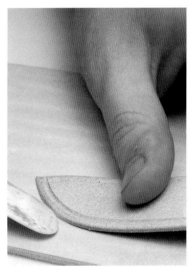

After the contact adhesive dries, glue the belt loop.

Remove excess glue with the bone folder.

We mark the width of the belt loop, i.e. we set the distance between seam and interior bend to about 1.771" (45 mm). With the V gouge we shape the groove for the seam, then mark the space between stitches with the space marker. We set the corners with the scratch awl to connect the lines. The stitches on the seam line are shifted at an angle of 30° apart from each other. Thus the leather won't be cut apart by the thread. On the backside we also embed the seam.

First we draw the width of the passage for the belt.

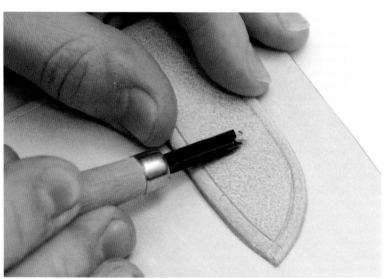

Then we cut the groove for the seam with the V gouge.

Cut the holes for the seam with the scratch awl. The awl has to be held precisely vertical while doing this.

The distance for the stitches is marked with the space marker.

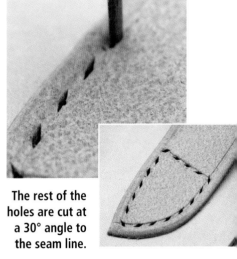

First we cut the corner holes in a way to connect the seam lines.

The rest of the holes are cut at a 30° angle to the seam line.

For sewing on the belt loop we need about 1.6 feet (0.5 m) of sewing yarn. We use black braided yarn. The seam is sewed with the so-called saddle stitch. We sew with two harness needles, one at each end of the thread. Harness needles don't have a pointed tip, so they won't cut through the yarn while sewing back in the opposite direction. To prevent the yarn from slipping off the needle, a special technique is used for threading the needle (see following page).

THREADING THE NEEDLE

To prevent the needle from slipping off the thread, a special technique is used for threading the needle. For this, the yarn to be used for sewing is first cut to size. In general, the thread has to be eight to ten times the length of the distance which has to be sewn. This means: for a seam 7.87" (20 cm) in length you need almost 6.5 feet (2 meters) of yarn, for thicker material (more than 0.472" [12 mm] in thickness) you need even more.

First the thread is pierced with the harness needle (see pictures below). With the second stitch you pierce the thread about 0.393" to 0.787" (1 to 2 cm) apart from the first piercing. In doing so, you have to take care that the tip of the needle points in the direction of the long end of the thread.

The end of the yarn is then threaded through the eye. For this it has to be twisted slightly so the strands won't come apart during threading. In case of difficulties, you can use a threading aid.

Now the end of the thread is pulled towards the eye until it stops at the first piercing. The long end is also pulled over the eye, thus fixing the harness needle. The whole procedure is repeated at the other end for the second needle and we are ready for sewing.

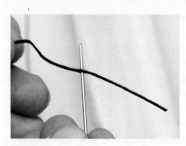

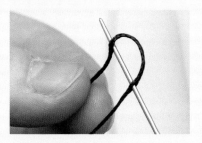

First the thread is pierced with the harness needle. One and a half to two and a third inches (4–6 centimeters) of the yarn are left over at the end.

With the second stitch the yarn is pierced about 0.393"–0.787" (1–2 cm) away from the first stitch. The needle tip points in the direction of the long end of the yarn.

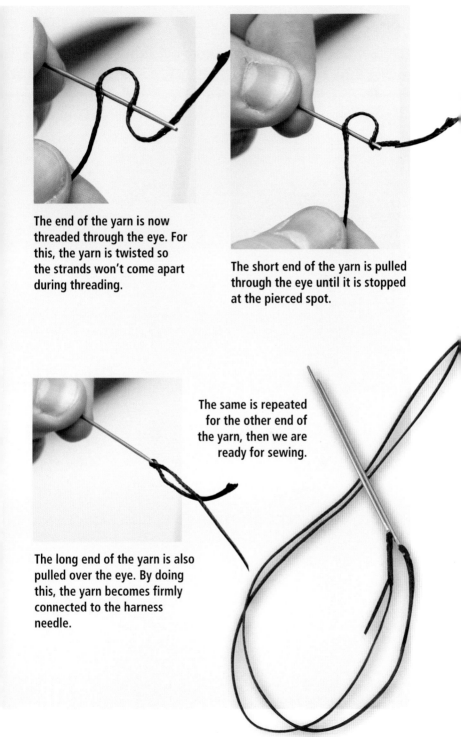

The end of the yarn is now threaded through the eye. For this, the yarn is twisted so the strands won't come apart during threading.

The short end of the yarn is pulled through the eye until it is stopped at the pierced spot.

The same is repeated for the other end of the yarn, then we are ready for sewing.

The long end of the yarn is also pulled over the eye. By doing this, the yarn becomes firmly connected to the harness needle.

We start sewing at the hole in the upper left corner (when looking at the side with the belt loop). We push the first needle through the hole and pull until both ends of the thread are of equal length. Then we push the first needle through the second hole and pull the thread through as well. After that we stick the second needle through the second hole, but from the inside, and drag the thread along too.

We push the needle through the rear, upper hole, then pull the yarn until both ends are of equal length.

We push the needle through the second hole...

...then pull the yarn to the flesh side of the leather.

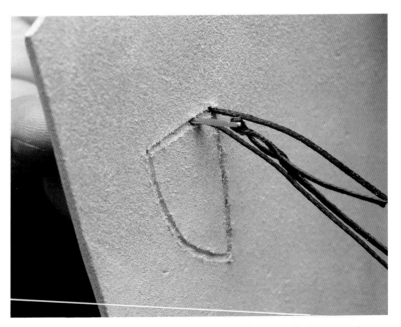

With the second needle we push from the inside through the second hole, passing the thread of the first needle.

With the first needle in the left hand and the second needle in the right hand we pull at the yarn to tighten it. The thread should sit tight but not cut the leather. It is ideal for the yarn to retreat back into the leather a bit.

We continue with the sequence of stitches until we are back at the starting point. The end of the thread which ended up outside is pushed through the leather once more so that both ends are on the inside. We tighten the thread once more, then cut the ends to a length of 0.118" to 0.157" (3 to 4 mm). The projecting ends are melted and welded by means of a cigarette lighter. Now the seam is protected from fringing and coming apart.

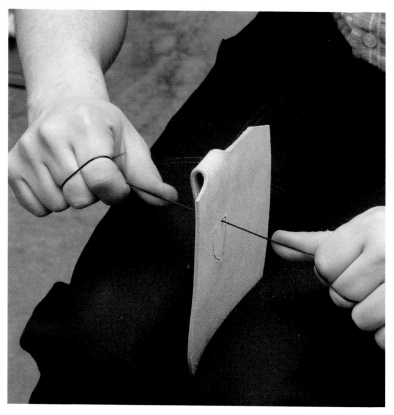

With even force we pull at the yarn to tighten it.

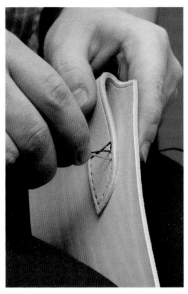

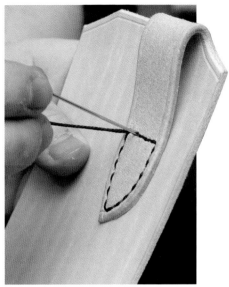

We repeat the procedure for every stitch, sewing on the belt loop.

Back at the starting point, we once again stitch through the second hole from the outside.

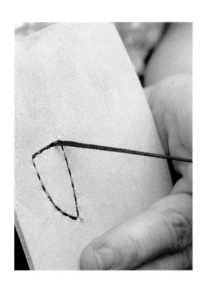

The yarn is pulled through and tightened.

Cut the yarn with the shoemaker's knife so there is about 0.118" to 0.157" (3 to 4 mm) left.

 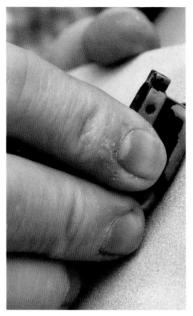

The protruding ends are melted with a cigarette lighter.

Press the hot liquid ends of the plastic flat.

The seam ends are welded in—nothing can come loose again.

2.5 Adjusting and Gluing the Welt

For constructing the welt, which has to protect the seam from the sharp knife edge, we chose a piece of smooth, full-grain leather the thickness of the blade (about 0.118" to 0.137" [3.0 to 3.5 mm]). From this we cut a strip with a width between 0.472" and 0.59" (12 and 15 mm) and a length which is slightly longer than the entire sheath. This should project a bit past the front tip of the sheath. With the shoemaker's knife we roughen the surface of the strip so it is easier to glue together.

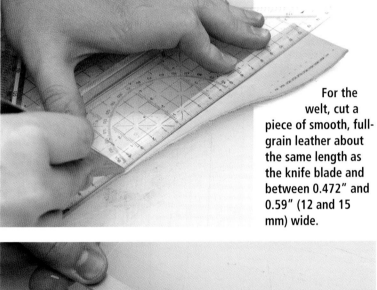

For the welt, cut a piece of smooth, full-grain leather about the same length as the knife blade and between 0.472" and 0.59" (12 and 15 mm) wide.

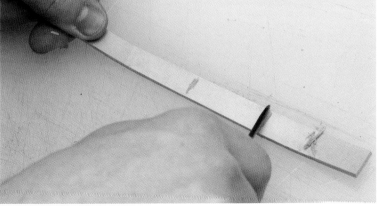

The grain side is roughened with the shoemaker's knife so it is easier for the contact glue to adhere.

We fold the sheath blade, put the knife inside, and check the dimensions of the welt. At the tip of the sheath we shorten the welt with a bevel cut so it fits cleanly. Then the position of the welt is marked on the inside of the sheath blade. We spread contact adhesive onto the marked area on one side of the sheath blade and the corresponding side of the welt, then let it dry. When the contact adhesive is tacky, we press the parts together.

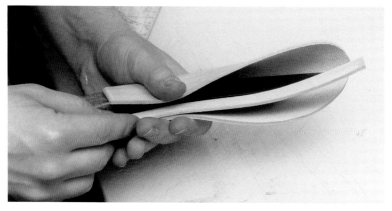

Put the welt into the sheath blade and adjust the shape to the blade contour by bending.

Adjust the tip of the welt and cut it off at an angle.

Mark the position of the welt with a pen.

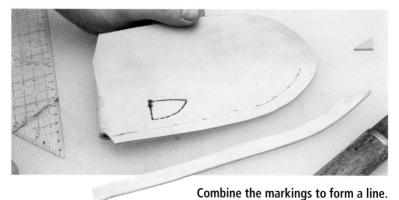

Combine the markings to form a line.

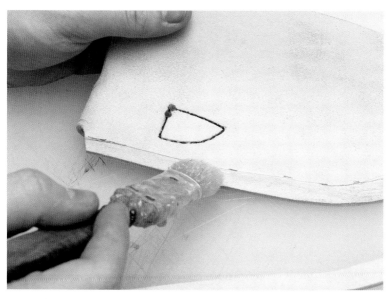

Cover the inside of the leather with contact adhesive along the line.

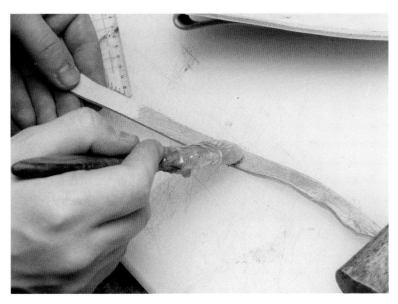

Cover the underside of the welt with contact adhesive as well.

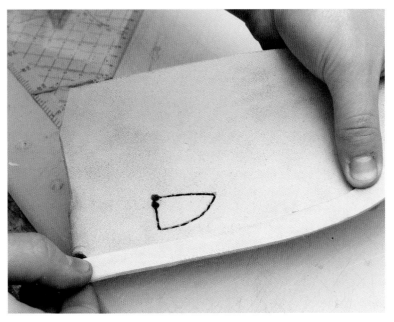

After the contact adhesive dries, glue both parts together.

The knife is then put into the sheath and the contour of the welt is transferred to the opposite side of the sheath blade. Both sides are painted with contact adhesive. After the glue has dried, the projecting part of the welt is cut off flush at the sheath opening. Now both sides of the sheath are pressed together, beginning at the neck of the sheath. We move towards the tip while taking care not to twist the sheath in the process.

Check that the welt fits correctly.

Mark the gluing position on the opposite side of the sheath blade.

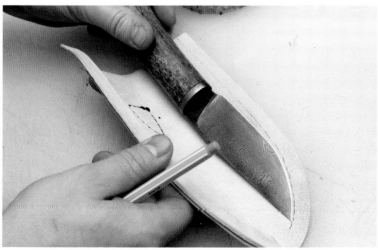

Paint the areas to be glued with contact adhesive.

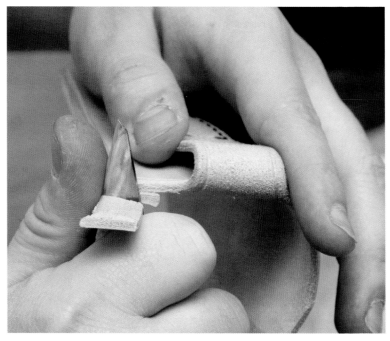

Cut the part of the welt protruding from the sheath opening with a knife.

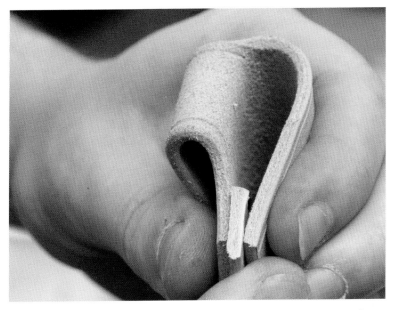

After the initial drying we press the leather parts together, starting from the sheath opening.

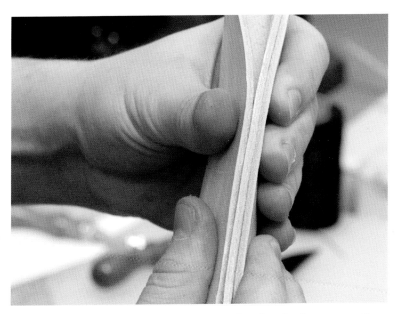

Step by step we work towards the tip, pressing the glued parts together.

2.6 Sewing Up the Leather Sheath

After gluing the leather sheath, we cut a groove parallel to the contoured edges of the sheath with the adjustable groover. For this cut we set the groover distance to 0.196" to 0.236" (5 to 6 mm), put the guidance pin next to the cut end, then cut the groove for the seam into the leather. With the space marker (distance of the spikes 0.196" [5 mm]) we mark the distance between holes starting at the intersection of lines at the sheath opening and work towards the sheath tip.

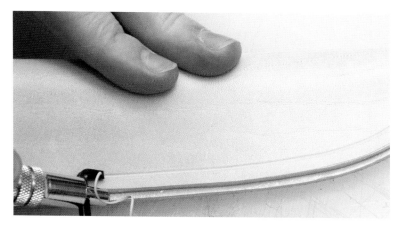

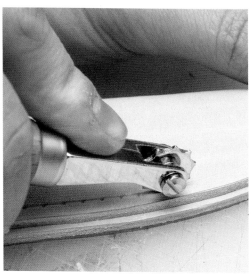

Now we use the adjustable groover, setting it to 0.196" to 0.236" (5 to 6 mm), and start moving toward the tip of the leather sheath.

The seam holes are marked with the space marker; the distance between spikes is 0.196" (5 mm).

The seam holes are pierced with the scratch awl while using a block of felt as a base. The scratch awl is turned slightly while piercing the leather (about 30°). The awl should be held exactly vertical while cutting the holes with it. When all the holes are cut, we embed the seam on the backside of the sheath with the V gouge. For sewing the seam we prepare 5 feet (1.5 m) of black, trout yarn and attach the harness needles—as is described in chapter 2.4.

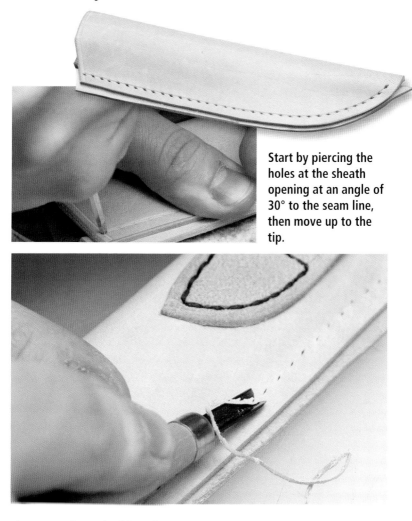

Start by piercing the holes at the sheath opening at an angle of 30° to the seam line, then move up to the tip.

The groove for embedding the seam on the backside is cut with the V gouge.

We start sewing at the third hole below the sheath opening. The needle is pushed through the hole and both ends of the yarn are brought to the same length. Now we sew two stitches with each needle towards the sheath opening, then back again until we reach the tip of the sheath. Since the opening has to endure the most stress, we have doubled the strength of the seam in this area.

After we have sewed the seam down to the sheath tip, we sew back one stitch with each needle, then add one stitch backwards with the thread end located on the front side of the sheath. Now both ends are on the back side where we weld the ends of the yarn.

We start sewing at the third hole. Since the greatest stress on the seam is in this area, we add a double stitch—first to the sheath opening, then back again towards the tip.

If the needle doesn't move easily, flat pliers without teeth are helpful.

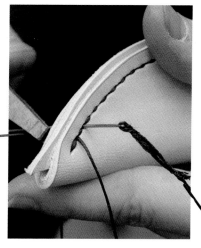

At the tip we sew one stitch backwards, then pierce through the third hole with the needle on the front side to bring it to the backside of the sheath.

Stitch after stitch we sew towards the tip of the sheath.

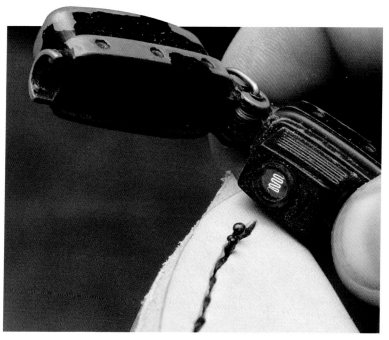

Once again we weld the ends of the yarn with a cigarette lighter.

2.7 Cleaning the Cut Edges

To achieve a uniform and symmetrical end on the cut edge of the sheath, we evenly cut off the projecting material with a sharp shoemaker's knife. Leave about 0.157" to 0.196" (4 to 5 mm) of material between the seam and the cut edge. Cut the upper end of the welt flush as well.

After that, we break the edges with an edge beveler (size 3). Round the corners inside the sheath opening. For areas that are inaccessible, we cautiously work with the shoemaker's knife. When everything is cut to size, we moisten the cut ends with a sponge. Once the water is absorbed, all cut ends are smoothed with the bone folder.

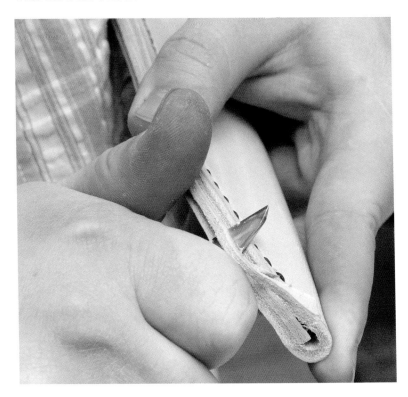

The projecting ends of the welt are carefully cut off with the shoemaker's knife.

The cut ends are broken with an edge beveler (size 3).

The cut edge at the sheath opening are also broken with an edge beveler from the inside.

Use the shoemaker's knife for sections that are hard to access.

Clean the transition to the sheath opening.

Moisten the cut ends with a sponge.

After the water has been absorbed, smooth the ends with the bone folder.

Also smooth the cut edges at the sheath opening and the belt loop.

2.8 Dyeing and Shaping the Leather Sheath

Before we start dyeing our leather sheath, we wrap our knife up with plastic wrap to prevent staining. For dyeing we use leather spirit dye. This kind of dye soaks deeply into the leather. Spread the dye thickly and evenly with a brush. We also dye the leather underneath the belt loop, at the cut edges, and the area around the sheath opening. Since the leather absorbs the dye quickly, we evenly apply a second coat until all the parts are colored.

To protect it from the dye, the blade is wrapped in plastic wrap. We cover the workplace with paper and wear disposable gloves. Then we start dyeing the sheath. The leather dye is applied liberally and a second coat is added if necessary.

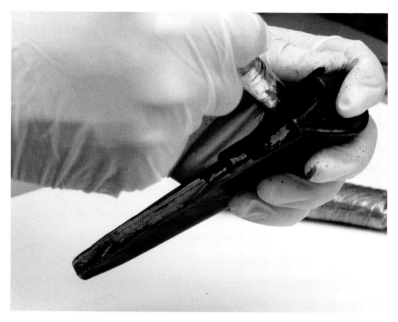

The leather underneath the belt loop is also dyed.

The front cut edge absorbs moisture at an especially high rate. Therefore the dye has to be applied several times in this area.

The inside of the sheath opening is also dyed to enhance the overall appearance.

The knife is put into the quiver-like sheath and the sheath is then shaped lightly along the contours of the knife handle. The cut edges are smoothed with the bone folder until they are shiny and have a level surface. The belt loop is also shaped with the bone folder so the belt will go through easily later on. Allow the sheath to dry for one or two days before we continue with our work.

Shape the knife's contour onto the moist leather with the bone folder.

Also with the bone folder, smooth the cut edges and make them shiny.

Shape the belt loop so the belt will easily fit through it later on.

2.9 Sealing the Cut Edges

Take the knife out of the dried sheath and once again smooth the cut edges with the bone folder. After that, we seal the cut edges, the backside of the belt loop, and the sheath opening with black edge sealant—apply several times at areas that absorb lots of moisture. The edge sealant then has to dry for two to three hours.

When the leather is dry, seal the cut edges with black edge sealant. For this, we apply the edge sealant several times with periods of slight drying in between.

The inside of the sheath opening is also sealed with edge sealant to prevent the knife handle from getting stained.

The other cut edges and the flesh side of the belt loop are also sealed.

2.10 Impregnating the Leather

To protect the leather, we impregnate it with leather grease. Leather grease is a mixture of various oils and fats as well as beeswax. It soaks deeply into the leather, making it supple and resilient. Distribute the leather grease evenly with a shoe brush. Underneath the belt loop and inside the sheath opening, use a finger to spread the grease. After a few minutes the fat will be absorbed and excess wax can be rubbed off with a piece of cloth. Inside the grooves and along the seams, use a soft toothbrush to remove the residue.

Apply leather grease to the dry sheath with a shoe brush.

Also, generously grease the inside of the sheath opening.

When the leather grease has been absorbed, rub the excess off with a cloth.

A toothbrush is helpful for removing the excess grease from areas that are hard to access.

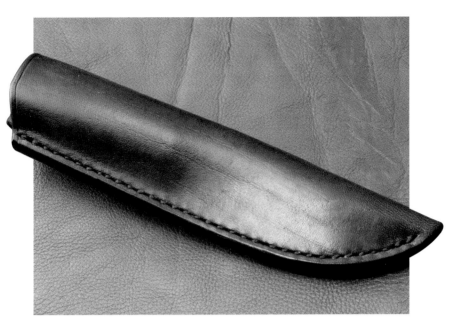

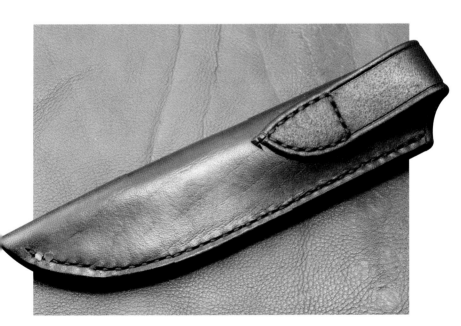

The finished piece: a beautiful quiver-like leather sheath with integrated belt loop made out of 0.098"–0.118" (2.5–3 mm) thick, smooth, full-grain leather dyed black.

PROJECT II:
QUIVER-LIKE SHEATH
WITH LEATHER LINING AND
RIVETED BELT LOOP WITH SNAP FASTENER

3.1 Planning and Design of the Leather Sheath

Our second project is a sheath for a knife with distinct guard and drop point blade. We construct a dark brown leather sheath of smooth, full-grain leather with a lining of black kid leather and a belt loop with a snap fastener. As we did in the first project, we start with a sketch of our planned leather sheath and draw our ideas on paper (a completed template can be found in the appendix).

3.2 Creating the Template

To create the template, we start as we did in the first project. The knife contours are again drawn along the centerline. We will use polished leather with a thickness between 0.078" and 0.098" (2.0 and 2.5 mm) and thin kid leather with a thickness of 0.019" (0.5 mm) for the lining. Thus we cut the measuring straps from the leather with a thickness of 0.098" to 0.118" (2.5 to 3 mm).

Start the template by drawing the centerline. Align the knife with the line and draw its contours.

MATERIALS AND TOOLS

Materials:
paper, letter size
smooth, full-grain leather, ~7.87" × 6"
   (20 ×15 cm), thickness 0.078"–
   0.098" (2.0–2.5 mm)
kid leather, black, about 6" × 6" (15 ×15
   cm), thickness 0.019" (0.5 mm)
brown, trout yarn, ~6.5 feet (2 m)
1 set of compression rivets with 0.236"
   (6 mm) head
1 set of snap fasteners with 0.59" (15
   mm) head
contact adhesive
plastic wrap
brown leather spirit dye
1 pair of disposable gloves
shellac dissolved in spirit
translucent shoe polish

Tools:
1 drafting triangle
1 French curve
1 pencil
1 paper scissors
1 shoemaker's knife
1 bone folder

2 harness needles, size 2
1 cutting board
1 adjustable groover
1 edge beveler, size 3
1 space marker, distance
   between spikes ~0.118"
   (3 mm)
1 compass with two needles
1 pair of pliers with smooth jaws
1 small sponge
1 drive punch, 0.118" (3 mm)
1 mallet (rawhide, wood, or
   plastic)
1 hammer (with polished steel
   surfaces)
1 tool for setting snap fasteners
1 base for riveting (e.g. a plane
   steel plate)
1 drill press
1 base for drilling (wood)
1 drill bit, 0.078" (2.0 mm)
1 V gouge
1 cigarette lighter
1 paint brush, width 0.393"–0.59"
   (10–15 mm)
2 pieces of lint-free cotton cloth

We measure the circumferences of the knife and add about 0.393" to 0.472" (10 to 12 mm) to each measurement, then transfer the values onto the template. Since the knife has a big guard, from that point on the width of the sheath measurement must not become smaller towards the handle butt because otherwise the sheath would be too small at the opening and the knife could not be placed into the sheath at all.

Design the outer contour of the leather sheath with an elegant curve, moving the sheath tip downwards to match it to the curve of the blade. The sheath opening also receives an elegant curve. After folding the paper along the centerline, we cut out the pattern.

Use a leather strap to measure the circumference. The strap is as thick as the leather for the sheath plus the kid leather for the lining.

The measurements of the circumference are marked on the template.

Connect the measurement points and draw the contour.

Now the template, which is folded along the centerline, is cut to size and unfolded. The template is finished!

3.3 Constructing the Belt Loop and Attaching it to the Sheath Blade

First we transfer our pattern onto the smooth, full-grain leather and cut it out. For the belt loop with snap fastener, we measure the width of the knife handle, then subtract 0.157" (4 mm). We draw a template, starting with a centerline. Then we draw a parallel line on both sides of the centerline. Their distance is half of the determined handle width.

For bending back the belt loop we need about 1.18" (30 mm). The loop ought to hold belts up to a width of 1.57" (40 mm). For the snap fastener and the tongue we need about 1.37" (35 mm). The measurements are transferred onto the template. With a French curve we round the corners and mark the positions of the rivet and snap fastener. After folding and cutting the template, check the proportions. The template is then transferred onto the leather and the raw parts are cut out.

Transfer the template onto the leather and cut it out with the shoemaker's knife.

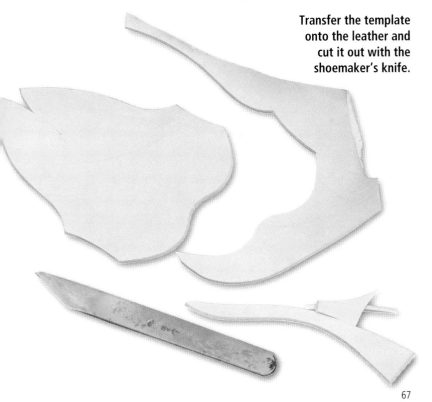

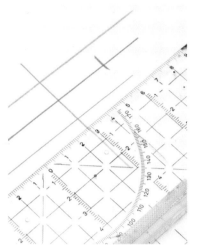

Measure the handle size to determine the width of the belt loop.

Design a template for the belt loop. For this we draw the width and the length.

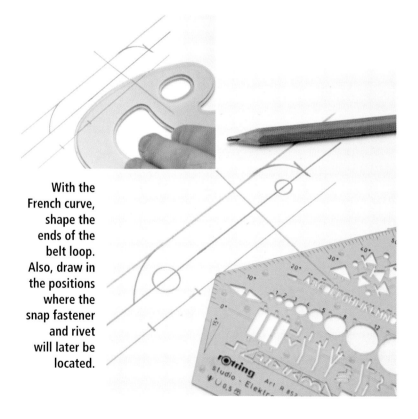

With the French curve, shape the ends of the belt loop. Also, draw in the positions where the snap fastener and rivet will later be located.

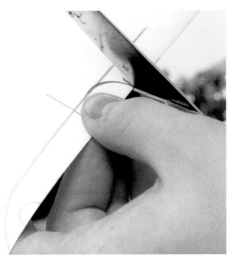

Fold the template along the centerline and cut out.

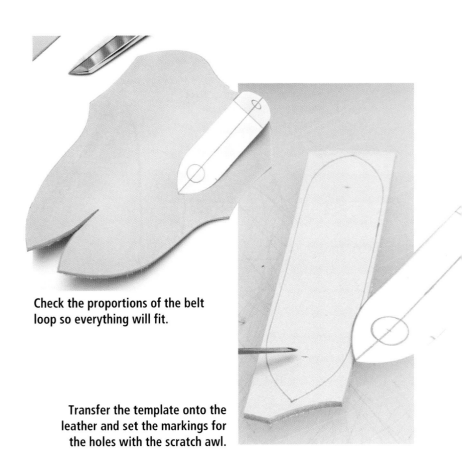

Check the proportions of the belt loop so everything will fit.

Transfer the template onto the leather and set the markings for the holes with the scratch awl.

With the adjustable groover, cut out a groove at a distance of about 0.118" to 0.157" (3 to 4 mm) from the edges of the belt loop. Break the edges on the front and backside with an edge beveler (size 2). Now moisten the leather with a sponge. When the water has been absorbed, round the corners with a bone folder or edge slicker.

The space marker can also be used for decorative purposes: With the spikes at a distance of 0.118" (3 mm) roll a mock seam. The holes for snap fastener and rivet are punched with a 0.118" (3 mm) drive punch. For this we use a rawhide mallet to protect the punch head. Use a plastic surface as a base. Set the snap fastener with a lever press. As an alternative, you can also do this manually.

On the belt loop, cut an ornamental groove with the adjustable groover.

The edges are cleaned with the edge beveler.

Break the edges on the flesh side of the belt loop.

Moisten the belt loop with a sponge.

Once the water has been absorbed, round the edges (here with a nylon edge slicker).

With the spikes of the space marker set to a distance of 0.118" (3 mm), roll an ornamental seam along the groove.

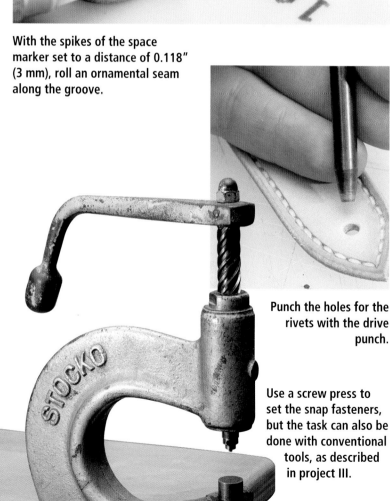

Punch the holes for the rivets with the drive punch.

Use a screw press to set the snap fasteners, but the task can also be done with conventional tools, as described in project III.

Place the second part with the spring washer onto the flesh side and flange the rim of the snap fastener with the screw press.

Put the top of the snap fastener into the hole.

Mark the position of the rivet, which will be used to fix the belt loop to the leather sheath.

Position the belt loop on the sheath blade and mark the hole for the rivet. Punch the hole with the drive punch. Now work on the upper rim of the sheath blade. Draw a groove for the seam and break the edges, then round these edges on the top side.

For attaching the belt loop to the sheath, use a compression rivet. It consists of two parts which are fitted together, then riveted. For riveting we use a base of steel and a small hammer with a polished head, which prevents the creation of dents and other defects.

Then we draw the position of the snap fastener and punch a hole with a diameter of 0.118" (3 mm). Thereafter we set the corresponding part for the snap fastener.

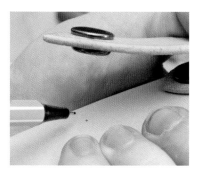

Bend the belt loop back and mark the position for the opposite part of the snap fastener.

With the drive punch and the rawhide mallet, punch the hole for the snap fastener.

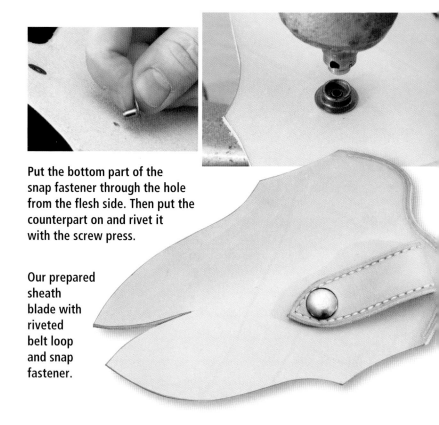

Put the bottom part of the snap fastener through the hole from the flesh side. Then put the counterpart on and rivet it with the screw press.

Our prepared sheath blade with riveted belt loop and snap fastener.

3.4 Gluing the Leather Lining

For the lining of our leather sheath we chose fine black, kid leather. Transfer the rough outline of the sheath blade onto the kid leather and cut out the shape. For gluing the lining, we use solvent-free contact adhesive. The adhesive is spread evenly on the inside of the sheath blade and the inside of the lining. After drying bend the sheath blade lightly and put the lining inside. Cut the excess material off with the shoemaker's knife.

The lining is made from thin kid leather. Draw a coarse outline then cut the shape to size.

Cover the inside of the leather sheath and the flesh side of the kid leather with contact adhesive.

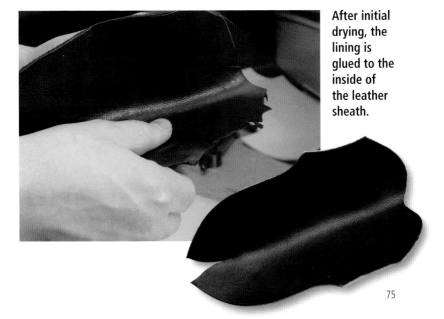

After initial drying, the lining is glued to the inside of the leather sheath.

3.5 Preparing and Fitting the Welt

We use smooth, full-grain leather with a thickness of 0.098" to 0.118" (2.5 to 3.0 mm) for the welt—this corresponds with the thickness of the blade. Here we also have to take the guard into account and give it space towards the back. To additionally secure the knife inside the sheath, we draw a little "nose" which is able to hold the guard in place. After cutting the main welt from the leather, we also prepare a small welt for the upper side of the blade tip.

Transfer the outline of the knife onto the inside of the sheath leather. The welt for the upper side of the blade receives a small V-shaped cut. Its length is adjusted in accordance with the shape of the sheath blade. Paint the marked areas on the leather sheath and the welts with the contact adhesive. After the initial drying, glue them in place onto the marking.

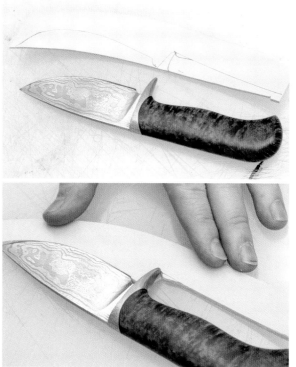

We make the welt out of a smooth, full-grain leather remainder. For this, the silhouette of the knife is drawn onto the leather. In the handle area we leave some space for pulling the knife, and past the handle guard we draw a small "nose" to hold the knife securely in place. Cut the welt to size and check its shape.

Another piece of smooth, full-grain leather is prepared for the upper part of the welt.

Fold the sheath blade and put the knife inside. When drawing the outline of the knife, be careful to draw the measurement of the handle guard at the sheath opening as well.

Now align the welt and draw its course onto the sheath neck.

Cut a V off the small welt for the upper part of the knife blade. This simplifies its adjustment later on.

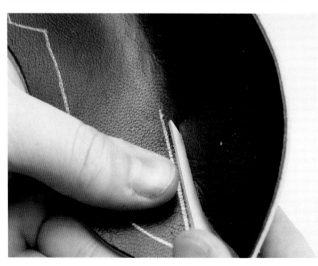

Check the fit of the welt and refine the V-shaped cut if necessary.

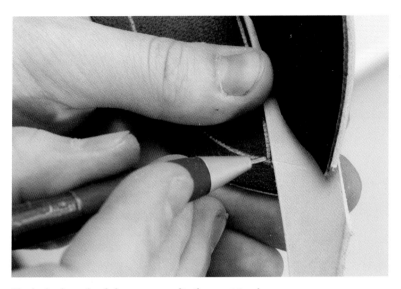

Mark the length of the upper welt, then cut to size.

After roughening the leather, paint the parts which are to be glued with contact adhesive.

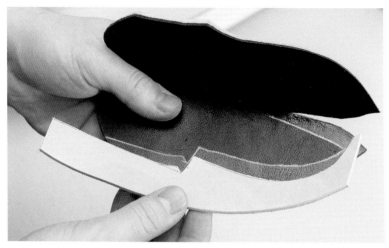

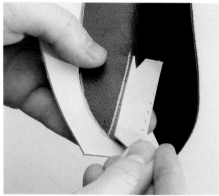

Start with the welt for the bottom part of the knife and glue it onto the marked area after the adhesive has dried.

The welt for the top of the knife blade is also glued.

Both welts project generously; the jutting ends will be cut off later.

We roughen the surface of the main welt, then put the knife into the sheath to draw its outline onto the opposite side of the sheath. After painting with contact adhesive and initial drying, we glue the leather sheath together. The projecting part of the welt is cut off.

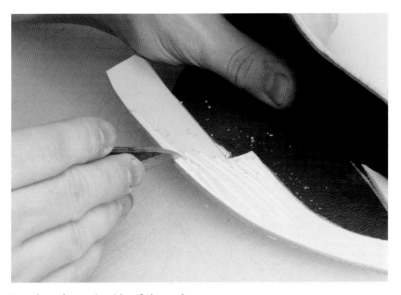

Roughen the grain side of the welt.

Put the knife into the sheath and transfer the position of the welt onto the opposite side.

Draw the contour of the knife onto the interior of the opposite side.

After roughening the leather lining, paint all areas which have to be glued with contact adhesive.

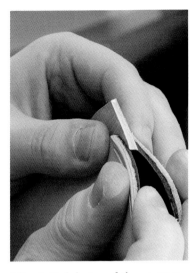

After initial drying of the contact adhesive, start gluing at the sheath opening. Be sure that the upper edges of the sheath at the opening are flush.

Piece by piece the sheath is glued all the way to the tip.

Coarsely cut the welt with the shoemaker's knife.

3.6 Sewing up the Leather Sheath

Draw the path of the seam with the adjustable groover. Use a compass with two needles to determine the seam holes. Adjust the spacing between the needles to establish the optimum distance between the holes.

For drilling the holes, we use a 0.078" (2.0 mm) drill bit. Put the leather sheath on top of a wooden base and cautiously drill hole after hole. On the backside of the sheath we embed the seam with the V gouge. Use brown, trout yarn for sewing up the leather. For easier handling, clamp the leather sheath in the vise. Use a thick piece of leather between the jaws of the vice to prevent damage to the leather surface of the sheath. Follow the instructions in chapter 2.6 for sewing up the sheath.

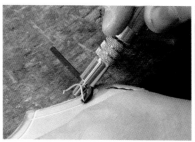

We again use the adjustable groover and cut the grooves for the seam. With a compass we mark the distance for the holes. If the distance between the holes doesn't divide exactly along the sheath, it can be enlarged or reduced accordingly until everything fits.

This time we drill the holes with a drill press and a 0.078" (2.0 mm) drill bit. This is a good alternative if you don't want to use the scratch awl.

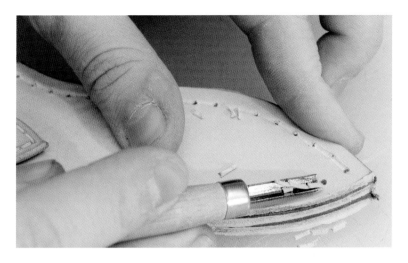

To embed the seam on the backside, the holes are connected with a V gouge.

For sewing, the sheath can be clamped into a vise with jaws padded with thick, soft leather. As described in chapter one, the sheath is sewed together using the saddle stitch.

3.7 Cleaning the Cut Edges

Grind the cut edges with a belt sander at slow speed and with fine grit to achieve a smooth surface. Clean the sheath opening with the shoemaker's knife and cut off protruding parts of the kid leather. Now moisten the cut edges with a wet sponge and smooth them with the bone folder.

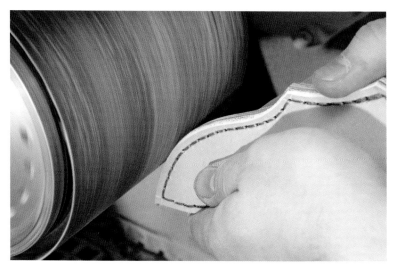

A belt sander with fine grit can also be used to work on the cut edges.

Here you can see the finely polished and slightly rounded cut edges.

Clean the sheath opening and cut off protruding parts of the kid leather with the shoemaker's knife.

Moisten the edges with a sponge.

Smooth the cut edges with the bone folder.

3.8 Dyeing and Shaping the Leather Sheath

For dyeing the sheath we use a brown alcohol-based leather dye. When the dye has been applied to create a uniform surface, the knife—wrapped in plastic wrap—is put into the sheath. Using the bone folder, shape the guard and the outline of the handle. Smooth the cut edges. Then allow the sheath to dry for a day or two.

After the knife has been wrapped and the sheath has been dyed with dark brown leather dye, we shape the knife's contours with the bone folder.

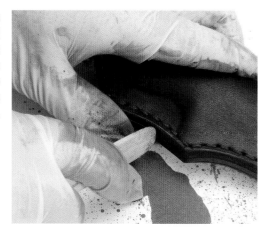

Smooth the cut edges to make them shiny.

3.9 Sealing the Cut Edges

When the sheath is dry we seal the cut edges with shellac. For this we use shellac dissolved in spirit and apply it in several layers with a piece of cloth until a slight shine becomes visible. After drying, we repeat the procedure three to five times.

For sealing the cut edges, this time we use shellac dissolved in spirit. This brings out a special shine.

The cut edges are treated with shellac and a piece of lint-free cloth. After drying, shellac can be applied in several layers until the desired amount of shine is reached.

3.10 Impregnating the Leather

To impregnate the leather and to achieve a beautiful shine, we rub the leather with colorless shoe polish. When it has been absorbed, we polish the leather to a high gloss. Remove the excess polish from around the seam with a soft toothbrush.

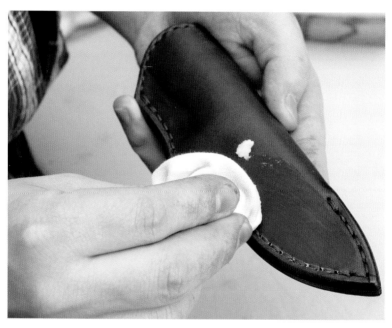

Use a colorless shoe polish to impregnate the leather. Spread it on evenly with a piece of cloth.

When the polish has been absorbed, remove the excess residues with the piece of cloth and polish the leather to a high gloss.

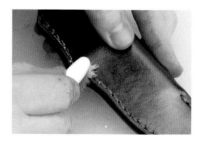

If some of the shoe polish gets stuck in the seam, remove it with a toothbrush.

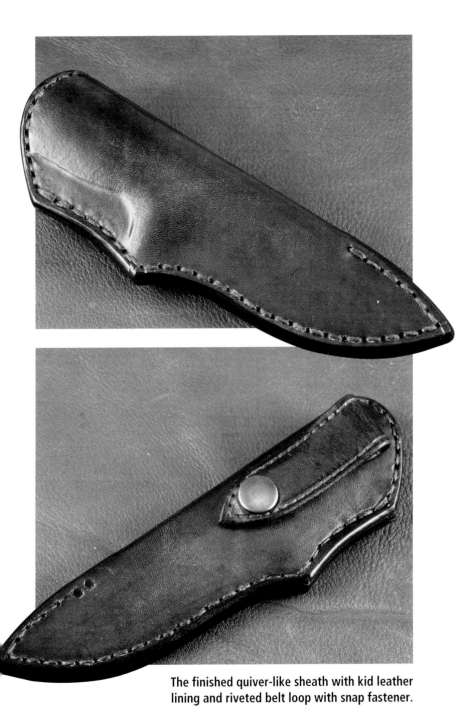

The finished quiver-like sheath with kid leather lining and riveted belt loop with snap fastener.

PROJECT III:
Quiver-Like Leather Sheath with Protective Strap and Sewed-On Belt Loop

4.1 Planning and Designing the Leather Sheath

Our third project is a sheath for a traditional Bavarian hunting knife. We will construct a brown quiver-like leather sheath of smooth, full-grain leather with protective strap and sewed-on belt loop. In addition, we will emboss it with a braided pattern and enhance it with a traditional finish. As with the previous projects, we first determine the design of the leather sheath and start by drawing a sketch.

4.2 Creating the Template

For this template (see appendix) we deviate a bit from the previous method because although the quiver-like sheath should reach up to the center of the handle, it should not close around it completely. We start with our template and draw the centerline and the outline of the knife.

We start with a template and draw a centerline onto the paper.

MATERIALS AND TOOLS

Materials:
paper, legal size
smooth, full-grain leather,
~14" × 8" (35 × 20 cm),
thickness 0.118"–0.137"
(3.0–3.5 mm)
kid leather, about 0.78" × 0.78"
(2 × 2 cm), thickness 0.019"
(0.5 mm)
brown, trout yarn, ~13 feet (4 m)
1 set of snap fasteners with 0.59"
(15 mm) head
contact adhesive
plastic wrap
brown antique leather finish
colorless leather varnish
1 pair of disposable gloves

Tools:
1 drafting triangle
1 French curve
1 pencil
1 paper scissors

1 shoemaker's knife
1 bone folder
2 harness needles, size 2
1 cutting board
1 adjustable groover
1 edge beveler, size 3
1 leather stamp no. X498
(basket weave pattern)
1 leather stamp no. C431
(camouflage pattern)
1 compass with two needles
1 pair of pliers with smooth
jaws
2 small sponges
1 drive punch, 0.118" (3 mm)
1 hollow punch, 0.78" (20 mm)
1 mallet (rawhide, wood, or
plastic)
1 hammer (with polished steel
surfaces)
1 tool for setting snap fasteners
1 V gouge
2 pieces of lint-free cotton cloth

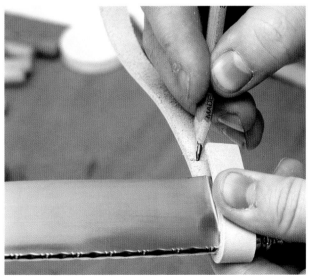

With the measuring strap we determine the blade width plus the seam allowance.

At the blade we measure the circumference, add an additional 0.393" to 0.472" (10 to 12 mm), and mark the values on the template. At the handle we only take measurements up to the lower edge of the handle (without the addition). Connect the paper markings and round the lines a bit. Now fold the template and cut it out.

The measurement of the blade width is transferred onto the template.

The circumference is measured at the center of the handle where the leather sheath will later end. Since the leather should be flush with the handle here, there is no addition for the seam.

Transfer the measurement onto the template at the corresponding height.

The second measurement at the handle is taken about 0.078"– 0.118" (2–3 cm) behind the guard.

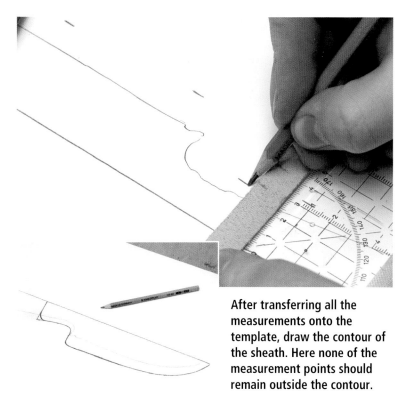

After transferring all the measurements onto the template, draw the contour of the sheath. Here none of the measurement points should remain outside the contour.

After folding the template along the centerline, cut it out with the scissors and unfold it.

4.3 Preparing and Embossing the Sheath Blade

Transfer the template onto smooth, full-grain leather with a thickness of 0.118" to 0.137" (3.0 to 3.5 mm), then cut out the sheath blade. To check the fit, place the knife into the sheath. Create a special border at 0.236" (6 mm) from the cut edges and a groove for the seam at a distance of 0.118" (3 mm) from the edge.

Now thoroughly moisten the leather and let the water soak in. Mark a line at an angle of 30° with the bone folder. On this line place the leather basket weave stamp and cautiously hammer it in. Work from the center towards the edges and set each stamp next to the one before until the whole surface is covered with a uniform braided pattern. It is important to make sure that your work is symmetrical and consistent. Set the camouflage leather stamp to achieve a uniform transition towards the border. Now shape the ornamental lines with the modeling tool. Then break and round the edges at the sheath opening.

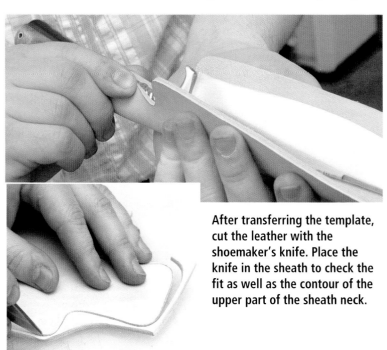

After transferring the template, cut the leather with the shoemaker's knife. Place the knife in the sheath to check the fit as well as the contour of the upper part of the sheath neck.

The grooves for the seam and the ornamental line at the sheath opening are cut with the adjustable groover. The seam is 0.118" (3 mm) from the cut edge.

Cut the ornamental line, which also creates a border for the embossing, at a distance of 0.236" (6 mm) from the cut edge.

Moisten the sheath blade on the grain side with a sponge and lots of water.

After the water is absorbed, draw a guideline for lining up the braided pattern.

Use a leather basket weave stamp for the embossing.

Place the long side down on the leather along the guideline and press it into the leather with a light blow from the rawhide mallet.

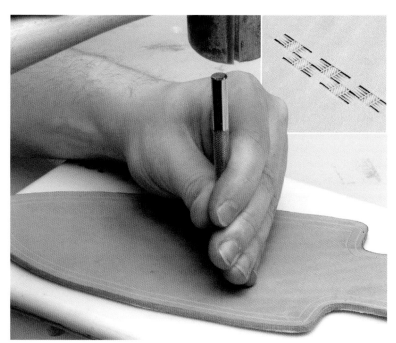

When embossing, make sure that the stamp is pressed into the leather at the same depth each time and one third of the long side of the stamp overlaps with the previous stamping.

Embossing with the basket weave pattern is complete.

Since the basket weave pattern can't fill the area completely, it is surrounded by a border of camouflage pattern.

The ornamental lines are worked on with the modeling tool to achieve a rounded transition.

Clean the cut edge of the sheath neck with the edge beveller.

Round the edge with the handmade modeling tool.

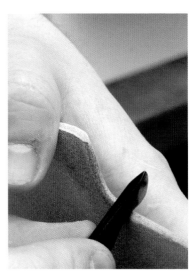

The cut edge on the flesh side of the sheath neck is also broken.

After moistening, smooth the cut edge once again.

4.4 Dyeing and Varnishing the Leather

We use brown antique finish for dyeing the leather. This creates an interesting two-tone color because the dark particles settle in the depressions of the embossed parts. The antique finish has to be shaken well before use and applied thickly onto the leather with a sponge. After a minute or two, wipe the excess off with the sponge. Allow the leather to dry for a day or two. After drying, seal the leather with an elastic leather varnish. The varnish protects the leather and prevents the antique color from fading.

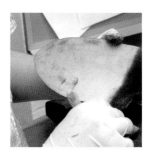

The sheath neck is also dyed on the inside.

Dye the sheath blade with antique finish to emphasize the embossing. After the dye has soaked in a bit, wipe the excess dye off with a moist sponge. The antique finish settles in the depressions and thus provides a nice three-dimensional contrast.

To protect the leather and prevent the antique finish from fading, the leather surface is sealed with a transparent leather varnish.

4.5 Constructing and Attaching the Belt Loop and Protective Strap

Before we start with the construction of the belt loop and protective strap, we set a snap fastener into the front of the leather sheath. For this we mark the spot where the snap fastener should be positioned. We place it centered, below the transition to the sheath neck, at a distance of about 0.59" (15 mm). Punch the hole with the drive punch and set the snap fastener with the marking punch. Use a steel plate as a base. To protect the knife blade from getting scratched by the snap, glue a thin piece of leather onto the snap fastener on the inside of the sheath.

Mark the position of the snap fastener on the front of the leather sheath.

After the hole has been punched with the drive punch, rivet the bottom part of the snap fastener. For this we use a marking punch with a plane steel plate as a base.

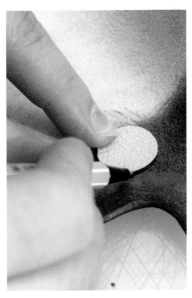

With a 0.787" (20 mm) hollow punch, create a cover out of thin kid leather.

Draw the outline of the cover on the backside of the snap fastener.

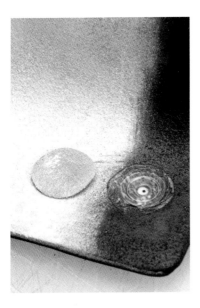

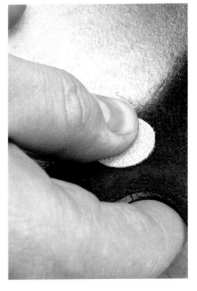

Paint the sheath and cover with contact adhesive.

After initial drying, glue the cover onto the snap fastener.

For the belt loop, first construct a template. The belt loop should have a width of 0.787" (20 mm) and hold a 1.57" (40 mm) belt. For sewing the belt loop on and bending it we need 1.18" (30 mm), as well as for the tongue. Transfer the measurements onto the drawing, round the edges, and shape the tongue.

Construct a template for the protective strap as well. Draw a centerline and a line parallel to it 0.314" (8 mm) away. Our strap will have a width of 0.629" (16 mm) at the transition to the guard. Shape the tip of the strap on the template with a French curve. Towards the rear end we add some more material for later adjustments to the strap. Fold the template along the centerline, then cut out the contours.

Measure the width of the sheath and decide on a belt loop which is 0.787" (20 mm) wide.

Make a template on paper and record the width of the belt loop.

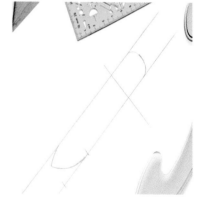

Draw the width of the belt and two tongues used for sewing the belt loop to the sheath onto the template.

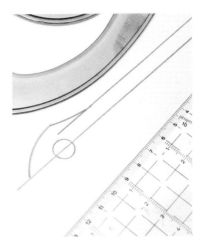

Measure the width of the protective strap.

Create a second template for the protective strap. Along the centerline, draw the width of the strap and the widening dimensions for the snap fastener.

Since we don't yet know the exact position of the strap on the backside of the knife sheath, we add a generous amount of excess material.

Now we adjust the templates to the sheath with respect to their lengths, we check their fit, and shorten them. Position the belt loop template and check the path of the protective strap. When the contours have been transferred and the leather has been cut, finish the belt loop because after that no further adjustments will be needed. We cut an ornamental groove, break the edges, and round them.

Mark the position of the belt loop with the help of the template.

Place the template of the protective strap centered on the snap fastener.

After bending backwards, the position of the belt loop is marked and the template is roughly cut to size and shortened.

Then the templates are transferred onto leather. Both parts can now be cut.

The position of belt loop and protective strap are checked once more.

Add ornamental grooves to the belt loop. Break and round the cut edge and round the inner groove with the modeling tool.

On the protective strap, only the top part of the snap fastener is set at first.

The protective strap receives a snap fastener. The snap fastener of the strap is fixed onto the sheath by means of its counterpart, then the strap is bent backwards. There we mark the width and position of the belt loop. To check, we put the belt loop on top of the protective strap. But prior to that, check their position once again.

The protective strap is connected to the leather sheath by means of the snap fastener.

Now it is fitted precisely and the exact shape of the strap is drawn.

The width is set flush to the belt loop.

Now the strap can be cut to its final size.

After cutting, we use the belt again on the leather sheath and record the length of the belt. The edges are broken and rounded. Check the position again, now glue the belt loop and the safety strap together.

When both parts are glued, we skive the bottom of both straps, now connected, and cut a groove for the seam. The exact position on the sheath is checked once again and marked.

Mark the upper edge of the belt loop.

Place the belt loop with folded tongue on top of the protective strap.

Fold back the loop and mark the length of the strap.

The areas which have to be glued are roughened and painted with contact adhesive.

Now dye the strap and belt loop with antique finish. Then, after drying, paint everything with transparent leather varnish. The leather varnish is elastic and is used for fixing the antique finish as this dye is water based and thus can fade. Now we glue the straps and sew them onto the sheath with brown, trout yarn.

When both straps are glued together, the transition is skived from below.

Cut a groove for the seam with the adjustable groover.

Connect the protective strap to the leather sheath with the snap fastener and bend it backwards. For gluing we add a third mark so the strap will have the right length later on.

The positions are marked once more for better visibility.

Sew the protective strap at its upper tongue.

Bend the belt loop downwards and sew it on.

4.6 Fitting the Welt and Sewing Up the Leather Sheath

For the welt we have prepared a strip of smooth, full-grain leather, 0.137" to 0.157" (3.5 to 4.0 mm) thick and about 0.59" (15 mm) wide. Place the knife in the sheath and mark the position of the welt. Then glue the welt onto one side of the sheath with contact adhesive. Now fold the leather sheath and draw the position of the welt onto the opposite side. After gluing the leather sheath, sew it up with brown, trout yarn. Cut the projecting parts of the welt flush to the sheath and clean the cut edges.

Cut the welt to size and glue it in.

Place the knife into the sheath and mark the position of the welt.

Cover the opposite side with contact adhesive and glue the leather sheath together, starting at the sheath neck.

Mark the distance between stitches with a compass.

Cut the seam holes freehand with a scratch awl. Make sure that the exit point of the scratch awl lies exactly within the groove for the seam on the backside.

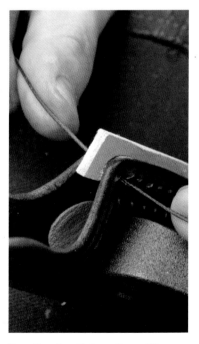

Sew the sheath together with a saddle stitch.

4.7 Dyeing and Varnishing the Cut Edges

The cut edges are also dyed with antique finish and, after drying, are sealed with leather varnish. Varnish the inside of the sheath opening to prevent the color from fading.

After the welt has been cut to size and the cut edges cleaned, dye it with antique-finish.

After drying, use the bone folder to polish the cut edges to a shine.

Seal the cut edges with transparent leather varnish.

Seal the inside of the sheath opening as well.

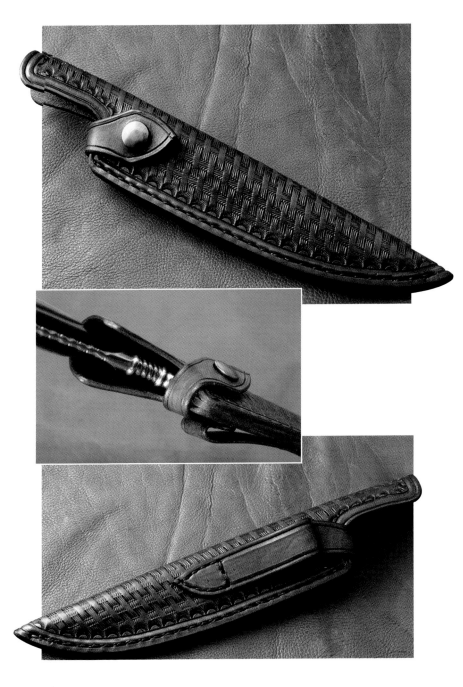

The finished piece: a beautiful quiver-like leather sheath with protective strap with snap fastener and sewed-on belt loop.

PROJECT IV:
Quiver-Like Leather Sheath
with Flap and Sewed-On Belt Clip

5.1 Planning and Designing the Leather Sheath

Our fourth project is a sheath for a flat, slightly curved knife. We want to construct a quiver-like sheath of smooth, full-grain leather with a flap locked by a snap fastener which will also have a sewed-on belt clip. As with the previous projects, we begin with drawing a sketch.

MATERIALS AND TOOLS

Materials:
paper, legal size
smooth, full-grain leather,
    about 15.7" × 7.87" (40 × 20
    cm), thickness 0.118"–0.137"
    (3.0–3.5 mm)
kid leather, ~0.78" × 0.78" (2 × 2
    cm), thickness 0.5 mm
artificial sinew, ~10 feet (3 m)
1 set of snap fasteners with 0.59"
    (15 mm) head
1 set of compression rivets with
    0.236" (6 mm) head
contact adhesive
plastic wrap
beeswax
leather grease

Tools:
1 drafting triangle
1 French curve

1 pencil
1 paper scissors
1 shoemaker's knife
1 bone folder
2 harness needles, size 2
1 base for piercing
1 cutting board
1 adjustable groover
1 edge beveler, size 3
1 space marker, distance
    between spikes ~0.196"
    (5 mm)
1 pair of pliers with smooth jaws
1 small sponge
1 drive punch, 0.118" (3 mm)
1 mallet (rawhide, wood,
    or plastic)
1 tool for setting snap fasteners
1 V gouge
1 cigarette lighter
1 piece of cotton cloth

5.2 Creating the Template

The template (see appendix) is based on the, by now, well-known principle, but it is extended with the flap. The flap provides additional protection from losing the knife. We start by drawing a centerline and the outline of the knife. The measurements of the circumference plus an additional 0.393" to 0.472" (10 to 12 mm) are entered and connected. The tip of the sheath is shaped in accordance with the outline of the knife blade.

For the flap we also draw a template which is shaped slightly conically and is about 0.393" (10 mm) smaller than half of the measurement at the sheath opening. We measure the required length at the flap and draw it onto the template. The curve of the sheath opening is drawn on the opposite side. Now we round the transitions. Then we fold the template and cut it out.

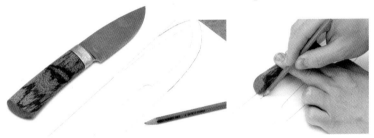

We start the template as with the previous projects. Since this leather sheath will have a protective flap which extends over the entire width of the sheath, the partial circumference of the handle is measured and drawn onto the template.

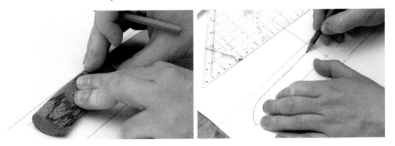

Mark the handle butt. The length and outline of the protective flap are drawn onto the sheath. For this a template is helpful. Determine the length of the protective flap with the leather measuring strap.

Draw the upper edge of the sheath opening and the transition towards the protective flap.

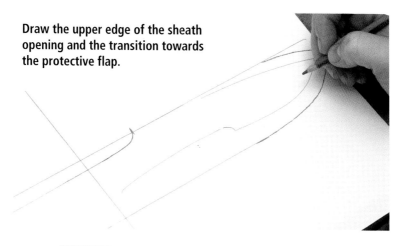

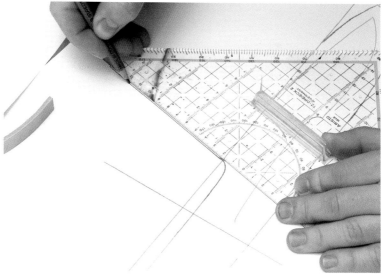

Draw the upper edge of the sheath opening on the opposite side with a slightly beveled line.

Fold the template along the centerline and cut out the contours. Cut the second flap along the line of the sheath opening.

5.3 Constructing the Parts and Attaching the Belt Clip

Transfer the template onto smooth, full-grain leather that is 0.118" to 0.137" (3.0 to 3.5 mm) thick and cut out the sheath blade. Construct another template for the leather mount for the belt clip and fit it to the sheath. We transfer the template onto smooth, full-grain leather, 0.078" to 0.098" (2.0 to 2.5 mm) thick, and cut it out.

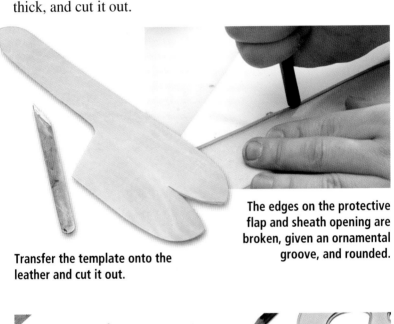

The edges on the protective flap and sheath opening are broken, given an ornamental groove, and rounded.

Transfer the template onto the leather and cut it out.

For fixing the leather sheath to a belt we incorporate a clip. Draw a sketch for the template of the clip mount.

A suitable distance is marked around the clip, the corners rounded, and the template cut out..

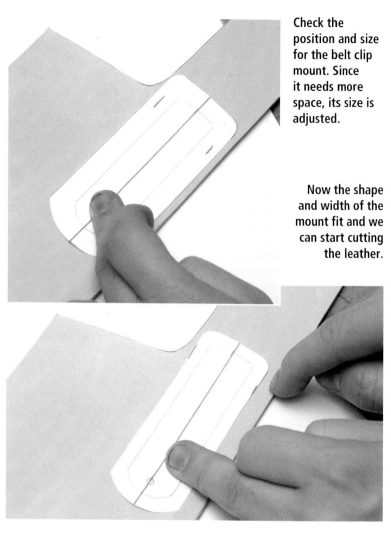

Check the position and size for the belt clip mount. Since it needs more space, its size is adjusted.

Now the shape and width of the mount fit and we can start cutting the leather.

After cutting the grooves for embedding the seams and working on the edges, draw the recesses for the clip. Punch holes with the drive punch, then cut the connections between them. The clip is threaded in, then riveted to fix it in place. We draw the position of the clip onto the leather sheath and tack it with contact adhesive. The distance between stitches is marked with the space marker, and the holes are pierced with the scratch awl. After embedding the inner seam, we sew on the belt clip with artificial sinew.

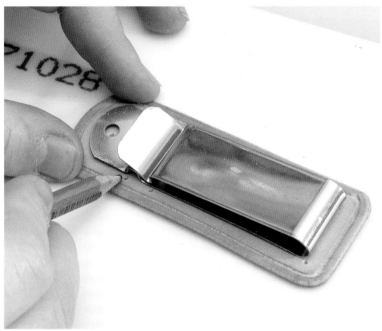

Put the belt clip on the prepared piece of leather. Mark the parts where the clip will later be threaded and fixed.

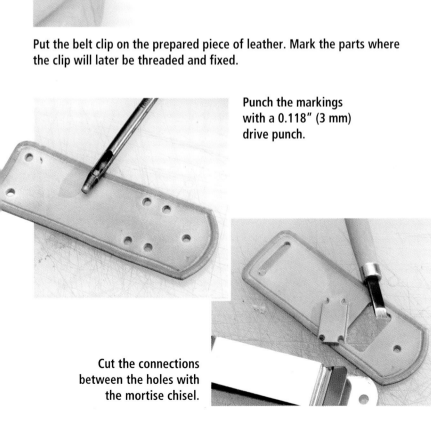

Punch the markings with a 0.118″ (3 mm) drive punch.

Cut the connections between the holes with the mortise chisel.

Here the belt clip is threaded in the leather mount.

Rivet the clip to the leather to prevent shifting.

The clip holder is marked and glued to the sheath with contact adhesive.

Mark the distance between seam holes with the space marker.

Pierce the seam holes with the scratch awl.

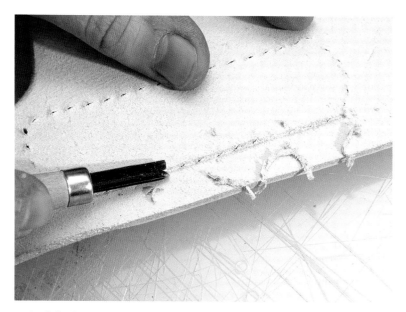

Embed the backside of the seam with the V gouge.

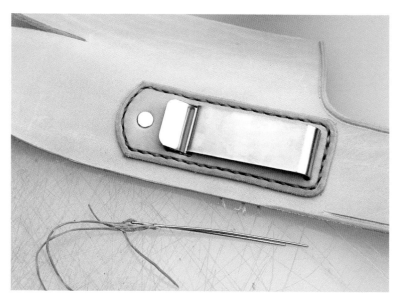

Then sew the belt clip to the sheath all the way around.

5.4 Positioning the Flap

On the centerline of the flap, punch a hole for the snap fastener. But before we set the fastener, we use the hole for positioning. Put the knife into the sheath and close the flap. This way the position of the snap fastener can be marked through the hole. The second hole is punched, and the snap fasteners are set. Once again we check the fit.

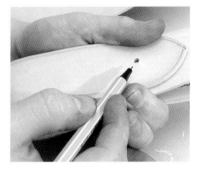

Center the position for the flap's snap fastener and mark.

After the hole is punched, put the knife into the sheath and transfer the position of the snap.

Punch out the marked position with the drive punch.

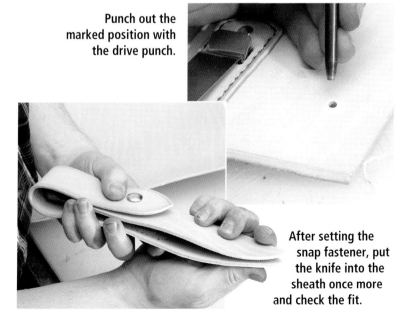

After setting the snap fastener, put the knife into the sheath once more and check the fit.

5.5 Fitting the Welt and Sewing Up the Leather Sheath

For the welt we cut a strip of smooth, full-grain leather 0.098" to 0.118" (2.5 to 3.0 mm) thick. First fit it to the sheath opening, then draw its position inside the sheath. On the back of the blade insert another welt. Glue the welts onto the sheath, put the knife back into the sheath, and draw its position on the opposite side. After gluing the sheath together, cut off the protruding parts of the welt.

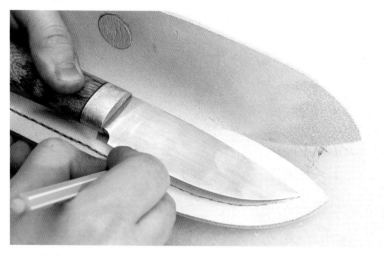

Open the leather sheath and draw the position of the welt.

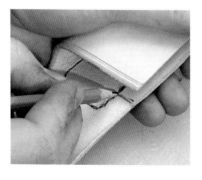

Put the sheath together and transfer the end of the sheath opening to the opposite side.

Fit the welt in, mark its end at the sheath neck, and cut it off flush.

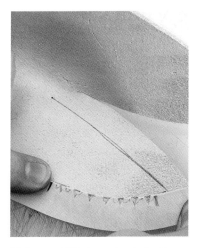

Make small V-shaped cuts in the welt at the curve of the sheath for better shaping.

Roughly cut the welt for the upper part of the knife blade to shape.

Skive the top of the welt a bit on both sides.

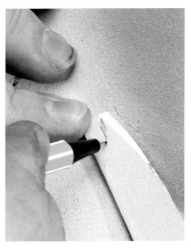

The bottom is beveled so the tip of the blade won't hit later on.

Glue the upper and lower welts.

After the opposite side has been painted with contact adhesive, the leather sheath is glued together starting at the sheath opening.

Clean the cut edges and cut the excess parts of the welt off.

Now cut the groove for the seam and sew the leather sheath up with artificial sinew. For better handling, we sew with the help of a wooden clamp which is held between the legs and keeps the sheath securely positioned in place. After sewing up the sheath we clean the cut edges.

After drawing and embedding the seam, cut the holes with the scratch awl.

To support the leather sheath during sewing, use a wooden clamp which is held between the legs.

As an alternative to welding the yarn, you can also sew three stitches backwards and cut the thread flush with the seam.

5.6 Sealing and Impregnating the Leather

For sealing the cut edges we use beeswax. Rub it onto all the cut edges; when polished with the bone folder, the beeswax melts due to frictional heat. Remove the excess with the ball of your thumb. For impregnating the sheath we use leather grease, which is applied thickly and evenly. After it has soaked in, rub the excess off with a piece of cloth.

After moistening the cut edges, smooth them with the bone folder until they are shiny.

Use beeswax to seal the cut edges, rubbing it into the leather vigorously.

Then polish the cut edges with the bone folder.

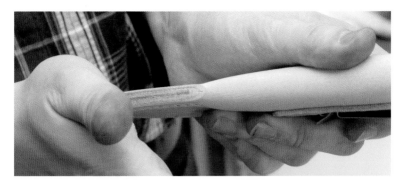

Remove excess wax by rubbing the ball of your thumb across the sheath with a bit of pressure. The friction helps the wax soak deeper into the leather.

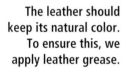

The leather should keep its natural color. To ensure this, we apply leather grease.

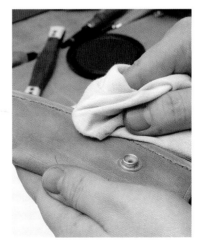

Apply the grease thickly to the inside of the sheath's neck..

After the grease is absorbed, rub the sheath with a piece of cloth.

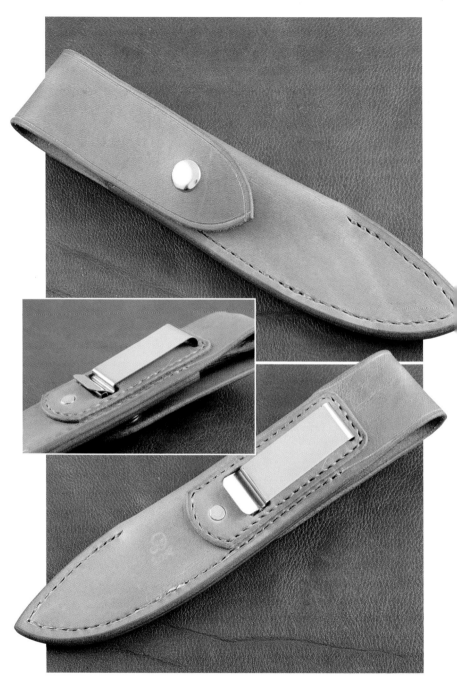

The finished piece: quiver-like sheath with protective flap and sewed-on belt clip.

TIPS
for Cleaning and Leather Care

From time to time a pretty piece of leather work needs a bit of care to stay in working order and remain good-looking for as long as possible. Therefore, here are a few tips related to this.

For drying, wrap the knife in plastic wrap and put it into the sheath, so the sheath keeps its fit while drying. A well-ventilated place with a temperature between 64°F and 77° (18°C and 25°C) is recommended for drying. It is strongly advised that you do not use a stove, hair dryer, heater etc., as this will lead to overheating which may cause shrinking, warping, and brittleness of the leather. After drying, the leather should be impregnated.

To protect the leather from external influences like dirt, water, UV radiation, etc. during daily use, it is recommended that you impregnate the sheath once or twice a year—depending on wear—with leather grease or colorless shoe polish. This protects the leather from drying and keeps it flexible. For this, treat dry leather evenly by applying grease or cream with a brush or sponge. If possible, rub it into the inside of the leather as well. When the agent has mostly soaked in, wipe off the excess with a piece of cloth. After treating the leather with glazing varnish a round of polishing follows.

This dirty leather sheath needs urgent care.

Remove coarse dirt particles with a moist cloth.

With a sponge and a bit of water produce a creamy foam with the saddle soap.

Rub the leather sheath vigorously with this foam.	Remove the soap residues with a moist cloth.

Let the leather sheath dry for a considerable period of time at normal room temperature.

TEMPLATES

Here are the completed templates for our four projects. The sketches are not printed to scale, but can be enlarged for your work.

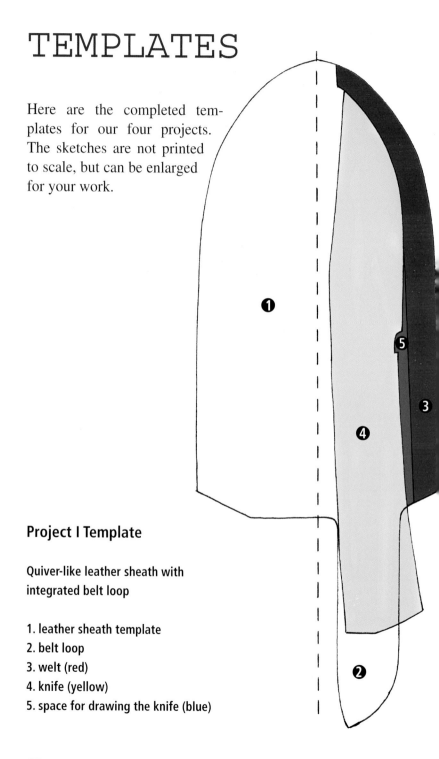

Project I Template

Quiver-like leather sheath with integrated belt loop

1. leather sheath template
2. belt loop
3. welt (red)
4. knife (yellow)
5. space for drawing the knife (blue)

Project II Template

Quiver-like leather sheath with riveted belt loop

1. leather sheath template
2. belt loop template
3. welt (red)
4. knife (yellow)
5. space for drawing the knife (blue)

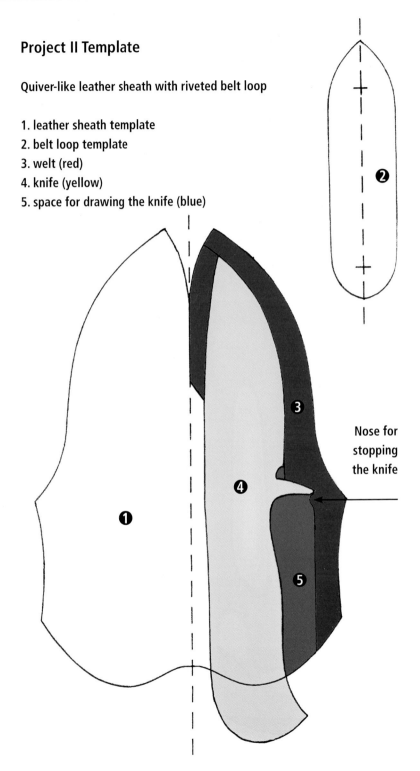

Nose for stopping the knife

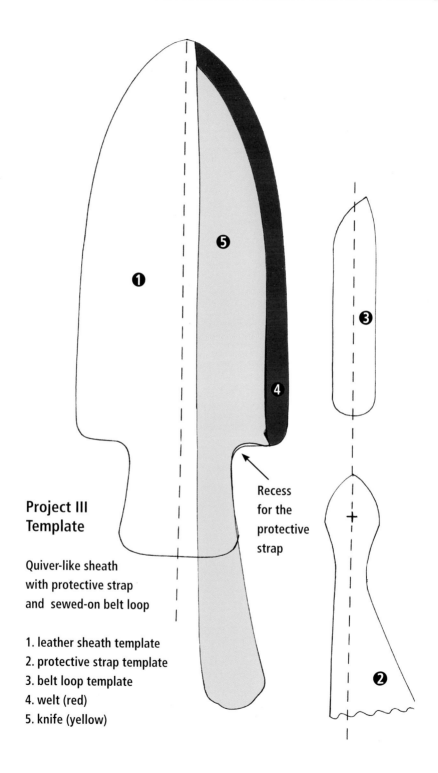

Project III Template

Quiver-like sheath with protective strap and sewed-on belt loop

1. leather sheath template
2. protective strap template
3. belt loop template
4. welt (red)
5. knife (yellow)

Recess for the protective strap

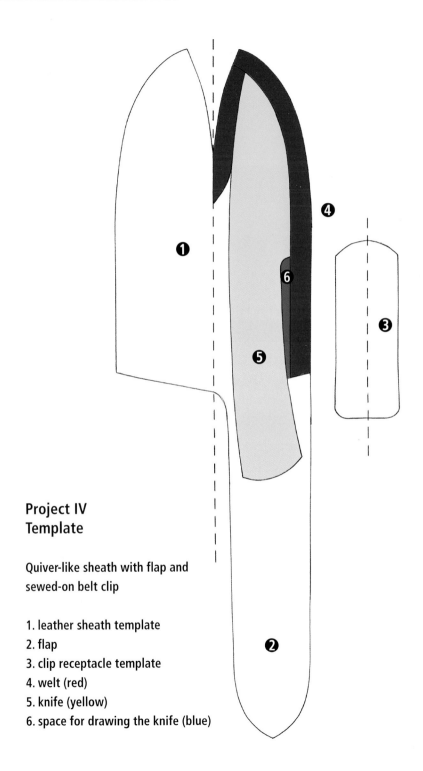

**Project IV
Template**

Quiver-like sheath with flap and
sewed-on belt clip

1. leather sheath template
2. flap
3. clip receptacle template
4. welt (red)
5. knife (yellow)
6. space for drawing the knife (blue)

LIST OF SUPPLIERS

These suppliers offer a variety of tools and materials.

Barry King Tools
(307) 672-5657
kingtool@fiberpipe.net
www.barrykingtools.com

Brettuns Village Leather
(207) 782-7863 and
(877) 532-8424
www.brettunsvillage.com/leather

C.S. Osborne & Co.
(973) 483-3232
cso@csosborne.com
www.csosborne.com

eLeather Supply
(877) 211-3489
www.eleathersupply.com

Hackbarth Tools
service@hackbathtools.com
http://hackbarthtools.com

Hermann Oak Leather
(314) 421-1173 and
(800) 325-7950
www.hermanoakleather.com

The Leather Guy
(507) 932-3795
sales@theleatherguy.org
www.theleatherguy.org

Leather Unlimited
(800) 993-2889
www.leatherunltd.com

Montana Leather Company
(406) 245-1660 and
(800) 527-0227
mail@montanaleather.com
www.montanaleather.com

Oregon Leather Company
(541) 465-9130 and
(800) 452-5058
www.oregonleatherco.com

Pro Leather Carver's Supply
info@proleathercarvers.com
http://proleathercarvers.com

**Sheridan Leather Outfitters and
Douglas Tools**
(307) 674-6679 and
(888) 803-3030
leather@vcn.com
www.sheridanleather.com

Tandy Leather Factory
(800) 433-3201
tlfhelp@tandyleather.com
www.tandyleatherfactory.com
100 stores in the United States,
Canada, Australia, and the United
Kingdom

Waterhouse Leather
(800) 322-1177
www.waterhouseleather.com

Wickett & Craig of America
1-800-TANNERY
info@wickett-craig.com
www.wickett-craig.com

Wild Mare Custom Leather & Supply
(806) 747-2320
www.wildmare.com

Zack White Leather Company
(800) 633-0396
http://zackwhite.com

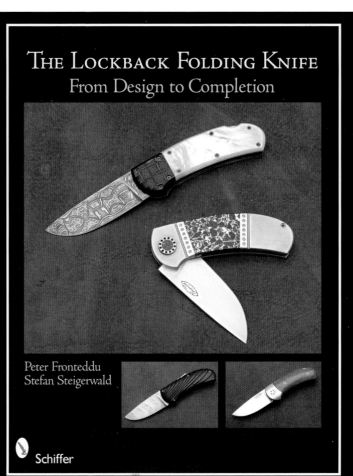

Basic Knife Making:
From Raw Steel to a Finished Stub Tang Knife.
Ernst G. Siebeneicher-Hellwig and Jürgen Rosinski.
In this book Ernst G. Siebeneicher-Hellwig and Jürgen
Rosinski show the simplest and least expensive
ways to construct a simple forge, make all necessary
tools yourself, forge a stub tang blade from an old
automobile coil spring, and make a complete knife.

Their practical guide dem-
onstrates the most impor-
tant theoretical basics and
shows how simple it can be
to experience bladesmith-
ing. Each step is presented
in text and pictures, with a
special focus on forging the
blade. Clear lists of tools and
materials help you through
the process. Practical tips,
explanations of terms, and
sketches round out the volume.

Size: 8 1/2" x 11" • 205 color images/10 drawings • 112 pp.
ISBN: 978-0-7643-3508-2 • soft cover • $29.99